Looking at Christianity

Michael Keene

ghton
HEADLINE GROUP

Acknowledgements

The publishers would like to thank the following for permission to reproduce material in this book:

Bible passages from The Holy Bible, New International Version by Hodder & Stoughton © 1973, 1978, 1984 International Bible Society.

The publishers would like to thank the following for permission to reproduce photographs:

All photographs by The Walking Camera (Alex Keene).

Every effort has been made to trace and acknowledge copyright. The publishers will be happy to make suitable arrangements with any copyright holder whom it has not been possible to contact.

Orders: please contact Bookpoint Ltd, 39 Milton Park, Abingdon, Oxon OX14 4TD. Telephone: (44) 01235 400414, Fax: (44) 01235 400454. Lines are open from 9.00–6.00, Monday to Saturday, with a 24 hour message answering service. Email address: orders@bookpoint.co.uk

British Library Cataloguing in Publication Data
A catalogue record for this title is available from The British Library

ISBN 0 340 73057 9

First published 1999
Impression number 10 9 8 7 6 5 4 3 2 1
Year 2004 2003 2002 2001 2000 1999

Cover photo The Walking Camera (Alex Keene).
Typeset by Wearset, Boldon, Tyne and Wear.
Printed in for Hodder & Stoughton Educational, a division of Hodder Headline Plc, 338 Euston Road, London NW1 3BH by Printer Trento, Italy

Contents

1 What's in a name?

What comes into your mind when you think of the word 'church'? A beautiful country church surrounded by a graveyard (see photo A)? A building in the middle of a busy city (see photo B)? A group of Christians, such as Baptists or Methodists, who meet together in a special building each week? All Christians around the world – about 1250 million of them – who belong to the Christian Church? All of these answers are right.

The early Christians expected Jesus to return to earth at any time. They didn't think they had time to build churches. Jesus, however, did not return. More and more people were becoming Christians and the existing buildings were not large enough to take them all. Also, the Romans became more friendly to the Christians. One emperor, Constantine, even became a Christian. So the Christians began to build churches in which to meet.

In the beginning

When the Christian Church began 2000 years ago it did not have any buildings of its own. The first Christians met together in each other's homes. They were in no hurry to build churches. It was dangerous in those days to be a Christian. Building churches would only have drawn the attention of the Roman authorities to them. Some Christians have started meeting in each other's homes again. They call themselves 'House Churches'.

A This church has stood at the heart of its village for centuries. Why do you think that many of the people who live here love their old church?

Churches

There is a church in almost every town and village in this country – and sometimes more than one. There are some cities like York, Cambridge and Bath where you seem to come across a church around almost every street-corner! Many of the churches are very old although others have been built recently. Churches are built for two reasons:

a To provide a place for people to worship God. If you go into an old church you can often feel that people have worshipped there for centuries. You can almost hear them singing and praying – in Latin!

B *Many of the people who used to live around this church have moved away. Where do you think the people come from to worship in this church?*

b To express how people think and feel about God. Almost every part of a church means something. Find out about churches and you will begin to understand the Christian faith. That is what this book is all about.

They have said:

Alan, 14: *'I have always liked old churches. There is one in our village. So many parts of it speak to me about God. There are statues, candles and stained glass windows which help to make God real. The smell of the incense reminds me of the prayers that have been said there for centuries.'*

- Do you like old churches? If so, can you explain why?

Do you know?

- how and where the early Christians met for worship?
- why the first churches were built?
- the two main reasons why so many churches have been built?

THINGS TO DO

1 With a partner pick an area that you both know well. Find out the different churches in the area. Make a map and mark in the places where there is a church – providing a short description of each one if you can.

2 Discuss with some friends the word 'church'. Write down all the words and phrases that the word suggests to your group.

IN THE GLOSSARY

Altar; Baptist Church; Methodist Church.

2 Introducing Churches

There are thousands of churches in Great Britain. Almost half of them belong to the Church of England. About one million people go to these churches regularly. A similar number go to Roman Catholic churches although there are far fewer of them. The most important Church of England and Roman Catholic churches are called cathedrals.

Some people go to Orthodox churches and these are named after the country they come from – Russian Orthodox, Greek Orthodox and so on. Many people also go to smaller churches such as Baptist, Methodist and Salvation Army. These buildings are often called chapels.

A *How many things can you recognise in this church?*

The Church of England

Church of England buildings are called parish churches. The whole of England is divided into 'parishes' and everywhere is served by a church. Most parish churches have a vicar to conduct their services. The vicar can be a man or a woman in the Church of England.

Some of these churches are very old and were built in the shape of a cross. They have a square bell-tower and a pointed spire. The bells were once used to call people to church and to announce important events. Many people who do not go to church are still baptised, married and buried in their parish church.

Roman Catholic churches

Church of England and Roman Catholic churches often look similar from the outside. Newer Roman Catholic buildings, however, are often round. A crucifix or a statue of the Virgin Mary often stands outside.

Orthodox churches

The dome of an Orthodox church reminds people of the heavens stretched over the earth. The square shape shows that all people are equal in God's sight. The four corners of the church are a reminder that people come from all parts of the earth to worship God.

Nonconformist churches

Baptist, Methodist, Salvation Army, United Reformed, Pentecostal and Quakers are called Nonconformist Churches. The outside and inside of their churches are plain and simple.

B *What are the main differences you notice between this Methodist church and the one shown in photo A?*

They have said:

Anne, 14: *'Our Baptist chapel is very simple. The main feature is the pulpit. It is there that the minister stands to read from the Bible, God's Word, and explains it. This is the most important part of a service for us.'*

- What is the most important part of a service in most Nonconformist Churches?

Do you know?

- which Church has more churches than any other in Great Britain?
- what a cathedral is?
- what a chapel is?

THINGS TO DO

1 Pay a class visit to a Church of England church, a Roman Catholic church and a Nonconformist church. Draw a plan of each church you visit. Is there anything special/unusual about any of the churches?

2 Imagine that you are one of the following:
a A teenager.
b A mother with two young children.
c A married couple in their forties.
d An elderly couple.
What activities do you think a church could put on that might appeal to you.

3 Visit to an empty church on your own. Write a poem or description of your visit.

IN THE GLOSSARY

Baptist Church; Bishop; Cathedral; Chapel; Church of England; Crucifix; Methodist Church; Nonconformist Churches; Pentecostal Church; Quakers; Roman Catholic Church; Salvation Army; United Reformed Church; Vicar; Virgin Mary.

3 Dedications

Every church ('God's house') is dedicated to God when it is opened. It is often named after a saint (for example St John) or a mystery (for example 'The Holy Cross'). This is true of all Church of England, Roman Catholic and Orthodox churches. In older churches you will often find the name of its saint on a bracket close to the altar, over the porch or in the tower.

Patron saints

Many churches were built in Medieval times. It was believed then that the choice of a patron saint for a church was all-important. The people who worshipped in the church placed themselves under the protection of their chosen saint. People were sure that the prayers of the saint in heaven would protect them.

Many churches are named after:

a **The Virgin Mary.** No saint is more popular than Mary, the mother of Jesus. You will often see statues of her in church, or pictures of her in stained glass windows. She is shown holding the baby Jesus, following Jesus to the cross, standing with John at the foot of the cross or holding the dead Jesus in her arms. There are well over 2000 churches in Great Britain dedicated to Mary or 'Our Lady' as Roman Catholics often call her.

b **John the Baptist.** Many occupations have claimed the special protection of John the Baptist over the centuries. Workers in the wool trade, those who work with leather, workers with sharp-edged tools, bird catchers and also those who live alone have all placed themselves under his protection at some time. Many of these groups formed guilds (societies) in Medieval times. Churches were usually built through the generosity of local craftspeople. It is not surprising, therefore, that many churches were named after the patron saint of so many guilds – John the Baptist.

(A) St Peter. Many churches are dedicated to him. Can you find out who he was?

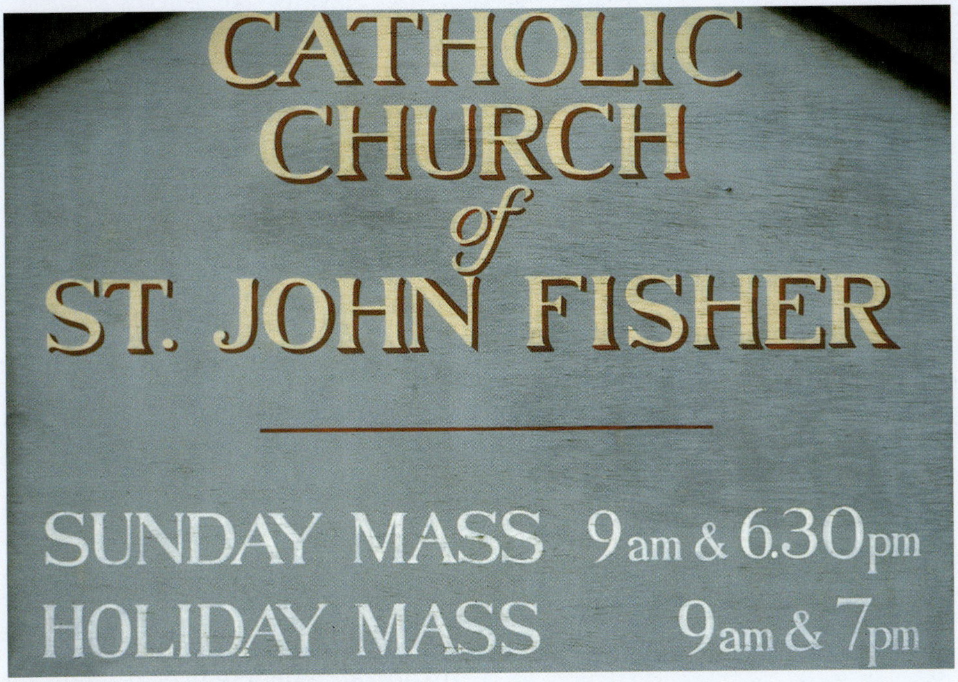

B *To whom is this church dedicated? Can you find out why this person is important?*

T THINGS TO DO

1 You will find a list of churches in your area in the *Yellow Pages*. Look under 'Places of worship'.

- **a** How many churches can you find dedicated to John the Baptist?
- **b** How many are dedicated to Mary? What are the different names given to Mary?
- **c** Are there any other saints who have more than one church dedicated to them in your area? If so, can you find out five pieces of information about the saint?

2 The four most popular dedications of churches are to the Virgin Mary, St Peter, All Saints and St Michael. Are there any churches in your area with one of these dedications. If so, invite the vicar of that church in to tell you something about the dedication of his/her church.

3 There are many churches dedicated to John the Baptist.

- **a** Who was John the Baptist? Write two sentences about him in your book.
- **b** Why were many churches named after him, especially during Medieval times?
- **c** Name four groups of workers who claimed to have the protection of John the Baptist.

? Do you know?

- what the word 'church' means?
- why people have dedicated their local church to a saint or saints in the past?
- why so many churches have been dedicated to the Virgin Mary and John the Baptist?

IN THE GLOSSARY
Altar; Anglican Church; John; John the Baptist; Orthodox Church; Roman Catholic Church; Saint; Virgin Mary.

4 Cathedrals

Wells Cathedral in Somerset is best known for the beautiful carvings around its main door. You can imagine what a tourist guidebook might say about it. '*The cathedral of Wells can be seen for miles. It has some of the most beautiful carvings and stained glass windows in the country.*' It would be right. Stand back and look at the outside of the building. It is an incredible sight. Go inside, look around and your breath is taken away. Many cathedrals are like that.

A *How would you describe the outside of this cathedral to someone who had not seen it?*

The bishop's seat

When the great cathedrals (bishop's seats) were built bishops were wealthy landowners. Sometimes beautiful churches were built in their honour and called cathedrals. In other areas the most beautiful church in the diocese (area) became the cathedral.

Each cathedral has a large chair, often beautifully carved in wood. This is the bishop's chair. He uses it when he takes a service in the cathedral. The practice goes back to early church services when the bishop always sat directly behind the altar. That is still where you will find the bishop's chair in a cathedral.

Cathedrals

The long passageway (nave) down the centre of a cathedral was often used by traders to sell their goods. A screen was put up at the front of the cathedral to keep the altar area separate for worship. It was called a rood screen as it often had a cross (a rood) at the top. Almost all of these screens have long since been taken down. Today people want to be much closer to the altar as they worship. New cathedrals, like Liverpool and Bristol, are round so that people feel part of the worship.

B *What are main differences beween the inside of this cathedral and a church that you have been in.*

There are services every Sunday in a cathedral. Some of them are taken by the bishop. The bishop also spends much of his time visiting other churches in the diocese. Cathedrals are also used for special services. People from all over the diocese come to these.

? Do you know?

- what a bishop is?
- what a cathedral is?
- why 'rood screens' were put up – and taken down?

T THINGS TO DO

Look at photos A and B before answering these questions:

1 Cathedrals are beautiful buildings. The best craftmanship was used to build them. Why do you think the builders took so much care over their work?

2 Why do you think that many Christians believe that a church should be as impressive and beautiful, as possible?

3 A building like a cathedral costs so much money to keep going. Why do you think that many people think it is worthwhile?

IN THE GLOSSARY
Altar; Anglican Church; Bishop; Cathedral; Orthodox Church; Roman Catholic Church; Rood Screen.

5 On Entering a Church

Water plays an important part in Christian worship. Inside every Catholic church there is a small container (a stoup) which is filled with holy water. The water is 'holy' because it has been blessed by a priest. People stop at the stoup as they enter the church to dip three fingers into the water. This reminds them of God the Father, God the Son and God the Holy Spirit – a belief that Christians call the Trinity.

A *Why is this person dipping her fingers into water as she enters church?*

They make 'the sign of the cross' on their body. They do this by running their right hand from forehead to breast, then from the left to the right shoulder. At the same time they whisper the words: '*In the name of the Father, and of the Son and of the Holy Spirit. Amen.*' The water cleanses them from their sins.

The sign of the cross is a reminder of the suffering and death of Jesus on the cross. In the past people crossed themselves when they got up in the morning and went to bed at night. It also became a means of making themselves known to other Christians during persecution. Now many Catholics sign themselves before carrying out a demanding action.

Genuflecting

Making the sign of the cross with holy water shows that a person is coming into God's presence. This action, performed as Catholics pass in front of the altar in church, shows the same thing. The Blessed Sacrament (the bread and wine used at Holy Communion) is kept in the tabernacle to one side of the altar. This shows that God is present and so each man bows and each woman genuflects in front of the altar (see photo B). When a person genuflects she lowers herself for a few moments on to one or both of her knees, looks up at the altar and crosses herself.

B *Why is this person going down on her knees in front of the altar?*

They have said:

Fiona, 22: *'When I come to church I want to worship God with my body as well as my mind. That is why I make the sign of the cross as I enter. The water symbolises the forgiveness from my sins that I need. It also reminds me that Jesus died on the cross so that my sins can be forgiven. Genuflecting in front of the altar shows that I am coming into the presence of God.'*

- Why does Fiona 'sign' herself when she enters church?

Do you know?

- what makes the water used in Catholic worship 'holy'?
- what 'the sign of the cross' is and when it is used by many Christians?
- what genuflecting is and when it is done?

THINGS TO DO

1 Look at the two photographs. Describe what the two people are doing. How do their actions prepare them for an act of worship?

2 Start collecting photographs/drawings showing the different actions performed during Christian worship. Add a sentence to each, explaining what is happening.

3 With a partner, think of four questions that you could ask a Christian, to help you to understand what making the sign of the cross and genuflecting mean.

IN THE GLOSSARY

Altar; Blessed Sacrament; Holy Communion; Priest; Stoup; Trinity.

6 The Sacraments

The most important Christian ceremonies and services are called sacraments ('holy mysteries'). The word itself really means 'a signpost which is pointing to God'. Each sacrament involves two things and the first is a bridge to the second.

a **A physical thing.** Sacraments use common, everyday things to help people understand spiritual things. So water is used in baptism; bread and wine in the Eucharist or Holy Communion; oil in anointing etc.

b **A spiritual meaning.** Each sacrament points to God. That is why the sacraments are important to many Christians. Without them they would find it difficult to understand many important truths. So:

- the waters of baptism show that sins are washed away.
- the bread and wine at the Eucharist remind people of the death of Jesus.
- the laying-on of a bishop's hands at confirmation passes on God's blessing.

A *At which sacrament do Christians make use of bread and wine?*

Sacraments

Just two Christian Churches, the Quakers and the Salvation Army, do not celebrate any of the sacraments. The Roman Catholic and Orthodox Churches celebrate seven sacraments as do some Anglican Churches. These are:

1 **Holy Communion.** You can find out more about this sacrament, which goes under several names, between Chapters 11 and 14.

2 **Baptism.** The Roman Catholic, Orthodox and Church of England Churches baptise babies (Chapter 7). The Baptist Church only baptises adults (Chapter 8).

3 **Confirmation.** (Chapter 9).

4 **Penance.** This is the sacrament of confession and forgiveness. People confess their sins and the priest promises them God's forgiveness (Chapter 20).

5 **Holy Orders.** Ordination is the service at which men, and sometimes women, become priests.

6 **Marriage.** (See Chapter 26).

7 **Extreme Unction.** Many churches hold special healing services at which those who are seriously ill are anointed with oil.

Most Protestant Churches only use two of these sacraments – baptism and the Eucharist.

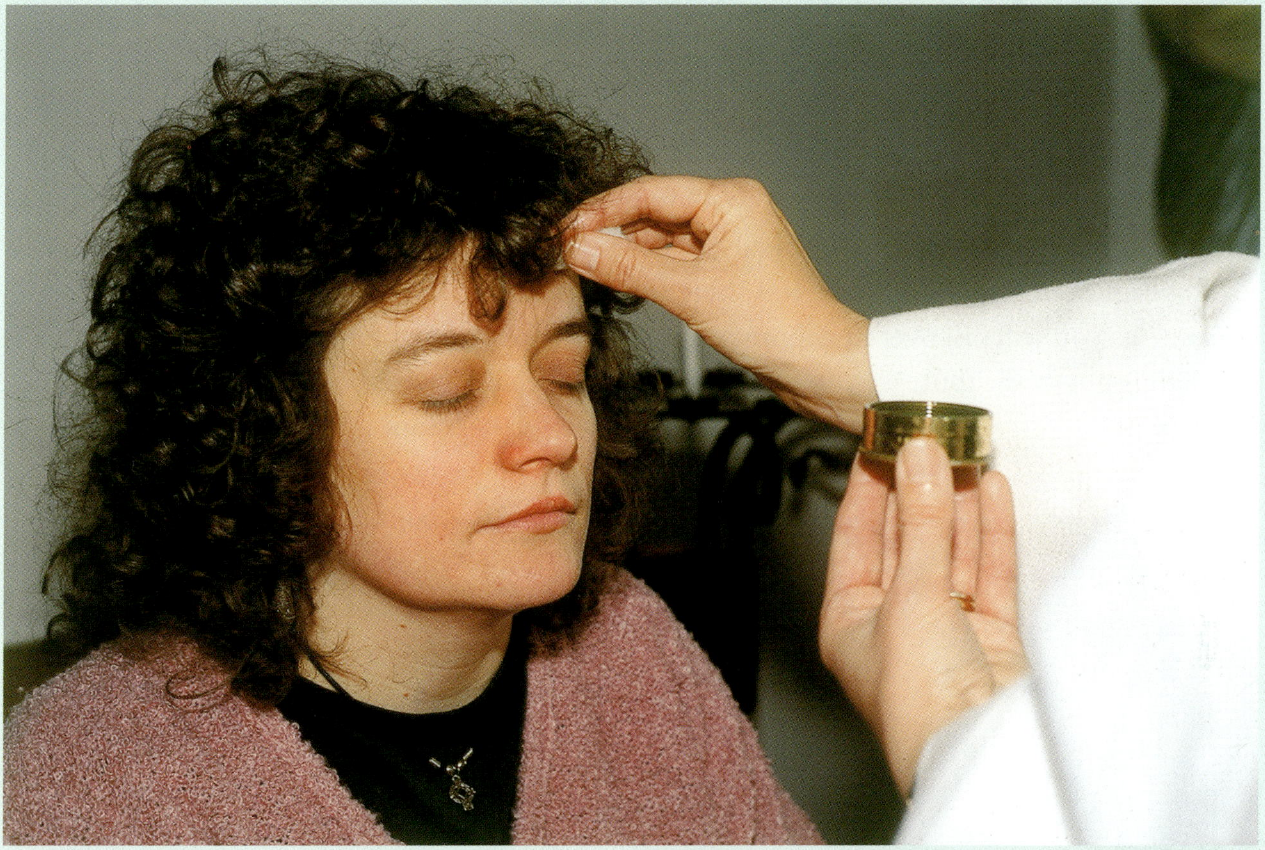

B *A sick person is anointed with oil. What do you think is the link between oil and healing?*

They have said:

Nick, 17: *'I do not find it very easy to understand God. That is why I need help, signposts to point me in the right direction. Some of the sacraments do this very well. The Eucharist, in particular, is a very important part of my life.'*

- Do most people find it difficult to understand God?

? *Do you know?*

- what the two parts are to every sacrament?
- which familiar things are used in the different sacraments?
- how many sacraments there are?

T THINGS TO DO

1 Signposts help people to find the right way to go. Sacraments act as signposts to help people grow closer to God.
   a Describe what a sacrament is.
   b Why do people need sacraments to help them to worship God?

2 The Orthodox Church calls the sacraments 'mysteries'. By using this word they are saying something very important about sacraments. What is it?

IN THE GLOSSARY

Anglican Church; Baptism; Baptist Church; Bishop; Confirmation; Eucharist; Extreme Unction; Holy Communion; Orthodox Church; Penance; Priest; Protestant Church; Quakers; Roman Catholic Church; Sacrament; Salvation Army.

7 Infant Baptism

You can hardly miss the font (see photo A) in most churches. It is just inside the door of all Anglican, Roman Catholic and Orthodox churches. It is there for a special reason – as you will discover in a moment. The water for baptism is put in the font.

A *What part does the font play in the service of infant baptism?*

To Christians, belonging to a church is like belonging to a family – God's family. They want a new baby to be welcomed into that family. The font is just inside the door of the church since it is through baptism that the baby joins God's family, the Church. Baptists, however, do not believe in baptising babies. They dedicate new babies to God. Baptism is kept until much later when the baby has grown up (see Chapter 8).

Infant baptism

For this service the parents, god-parents and priest gather around the font. The priest asks the parents and god-parents some questions before making the sign of the cross on the baby's forehead. He pours water over the baby's head three times as he says:
'I baptise you in the name of the Father, and of the Son and of the Holy Spirit.'

The water shows that the baby has been cleansed from sin.

B *What does the water that this vicar is using to make the sign of the cross symbolise?*

In Anglican and Methodist churches the parents are often handed a lighted candle during the baptism. They hold it for the baby as the priest says to him or her: *'I give you this sign, for now you belong to Christ, the light of the world. Let your light shine before men that they might see your good works and give glory to your Father who is in heaven.'*

? Do you know?

- which family a baby joins when he or she is baptised?
- why water is poured over a baby's head three times during a baptism?
- why a lighted candle is sometimes handed to the parents during the service?

T THINGS TO DO

1 a Look at photo A. It shows a baptismal font. Why is this font usually placed just inside the door of a church?

b Look at photo B. Name three Churches in which you could see a scene like this.

2 The service of infant baptism is usually carried out in front of members of the church. There is a good reason for this. Can you work out what it is?

3 Why do you think so many parents still want to have their babies baptised? Many of these parents do not go to church themselves. Is that surprising? Will you have your own children baptised? Explain your answer – one way or the other.

IN THE GLOSSARY

Anglican Church; Baptism; Baptist Church; Font; Infant Baptism; Methodist Church; Orthodox Church; Priest; Roman Catholic Church.

8 Believer's Baptism

Baptists do not baptise babies. They believe that no one should be baptised until they have their own faith in Jesus. A young baby cannot do this. The Baptist Church does not baptise anyone until they are at least 12 years old. In most Baptist churches there is a pool, called a baptistry, underneath the floorboards at the front. For a baptismal service it is uncovered and filled with water.

Some Baptists, though, want to follow the example of Jesus who was baptised by John the Baptist (see Information Box) as closely as possible. They are baptised in a local river or sea. Sometimes they go to the Holy Land to be baptised in the River Jordan.

A Can you think of one other Christian ceremony in which water plays an important part?

Believer's Baptism

For a believer's baptism, it is the meaning of what happens, and not the event itself, which is important. The service takes place in front of church members. Each person describes how they became a Christian. Three actions are then carried out:

Step One The person goes down into the water. This shows that they are leaving their old life behind them. Their sins have been forgiven because they have trusted in Jesus as their Saviour.

Step two The person is baptised by being rocked back beneath the water. This shows everyone that they have finished with their old sinful way of life. Jesus spent three days buried in the tomb after he died. Beneath the water they have been 'buried' with Christ.

B What is being recalled in the moment that the person spends beneath the water?

Step three The person comes up from the water and leaves the pool by a different set of steps. They have now begun to live a new life. After his resurrection from the dead Jesus was a new person. Now the believer can share this new life with Jesus.

C *What is this person determined to do as he leaves the water?*

Do you know?

- why Baptists only baptise adults?
- how some Christians try to follow the example of Jesus as closely as possible when they are baptised?
- what each person does before he or she is baptised?

INFORMATION BOX

'At that time Jesus came from Nazareth in Galilee and was baptised by John in the Jordan. As Jesus was coming up out of the water, he saw heaven being torn open and the Spirit descending on him like a dove. And a voice from heaven: "You are my Son, whom I love; with you I am well pleased."' (Mark 1.9–11).

- What did Jesus see when he came up out of the water?

THINGS TO DO

1 Look carefully at photographs A, B and C.
   - **a** In which church is this service likely to be taking place?
   - **b** Why do you think that those being baptised wear mainly white clothes?
   - **c** Why is it important for this service that the person being baptised is an adult?

2 In photograph C the person has been baptised and is coming up out of the water.
   - **a** Which event in the life of Jesus is suggested by this?
   - **b** What is this person indicating about their own life as they come out of the water?

3 The early Christians only carried out baptism in running water – whether in a stream, a lake or the sea. Can you think of one reason for this?

IN THE GLOSSARY

Baptism; Baptist Church; Baptistry; Believer's Baptism; John the Baptist.

9 The Altar

The most important item in almost all churches is the altar (table). The altar is the holiest part of the building, the place where the priest meets with God. The High (most important) Altar is at the east end of the church facing both the rising sun and the holy city of Jerusalem.

The altar

There is an altar in all Anglican, Roman Catholic and Orthodox churches. The most important acts of worship take place there. These include the Eucharist and Confirmation. An area in front of the altar is separated from the people by a rail. This area is called the sanctuary (safe place). Worshippers kneel at the rail to receive the bread and wine during the Eucharist.

A *The area in front of the altar is called the 'sanctuary'. Can you find out why?*

In some churches the altar is very simple, just a table with an open Bible and some flowers. The worship in these churches is simple as well. In other churches, mostly Roman Catholic, the altar holds up to six candlesticks and a crucifix. A crucifix is a cross with a figure of Jesus on it.

The tabernacle

In many churches some of the bread and wine that has been blessed in the Eucharist is kept for later use. Sometimes it is taken to the house of a person who is unwell. Bread and wine that have been blessed are kept in a small cupboard, called the tabernacle. This is found on the wall to the right-hand side of the altar. Different coloured lights are lit in the sanctuary to show whether or not the sacrament has been blessed. A white light shows that it has. Anyone who passes in front of the altar with this light showing should cross themselves, bow or genuflect.

B *What is the name of the cupboard to one side of the altar and what is it used for?*

T THINGS TO DO

1 Copy out this paragraph and fill in the missing words:
The holiest part of most churches is the ______. You will find an altar in all ______,______ and ______ churches. The ______is the area in front of the altar. The ______ is to the right-hand side of the altar and contains the ______ and ______ for use in the ______ service.

They have said:

Feodorov, 19:

'I worship in a Russian Orthodox church. I have always been taught to treat the church as holy. If God is there in some way then the place must be holy. The altar is the holiest place in the church. Only the priest is able to approach God at the altar.'

- What do you think Feodorov means when he describes his church as 'holy'?

Do you know?

- what the altar is?
- what the sanctuary is?
- what the tabernacle is?

IN THE GLOSSARY

Altar; Anglican Church; Bible; Confirmation; Crucifix; Eucharist; Jerusalem; Orthodox Church; Priest; Roman Catholic Church; Sacrament; Sanctuary; Tabernacle.

2 Answer each of these questions in just one sentence:

a Why is the altar the holiest part of most churches?

b Why is the altar found in front of the eastern wall in a church?

c Which services are conducted at the altar?

10 Confirmation

The same Churches that baptise babies also confirm people. In the Orthodox Church, infant baptism and confirmation are carried out in the same service. A baby is baptised and then confirmed. In the Anglican and Roman Catholic Churches people who have been baptised can return when they are older to be confirmed. In both Churches only a bishop can carry out confirmation (see photo A).

A *Why do you think it is always a bishop who conducts a confirmation service?*

Confirmation

When a baby is baptised, parents and god-parents are asked several questions. They answer these for the baby. Now, much later, the person can return to answer the same questions for himself or herself. At confirmation the bishop wants to know if they still believe in God the Father, God the Son and God the Holy Spirit.

When they have answered the questions the bishop places his hands on the top of their head. This is a very old Christian ceremony, going all the way back to the New Testament, called the laying-on-of-hands. By doing this the bishop passes on the Holy Spirit, and all his gifts, to the person. In the Roman Catholic confirmation service two other interesting things take place:

a The bishop makes the sign of the cross on each person's forehead with oil. The bishop is hoping that they will enjoy inner, spiritual healing.

b The bishop slaps the face of each person being confirmed lightly with two fingers. This is a sign that all the sins they have committed since they were baptised have been forgiven.

B *Where does the idea of laying-hands on a person come from?*

THINGS TO DO

1 In the Methodist Church a new member will sign a declaration which they then repeat every year. You can see what this declaration says in photo C.

a Who is welcome to become a member of the Methodist Church?

b This card tells us that each member of the Methodist Church must do seven things. What are they?

c How does each member of the Methodist Church show their faith to the outside world?

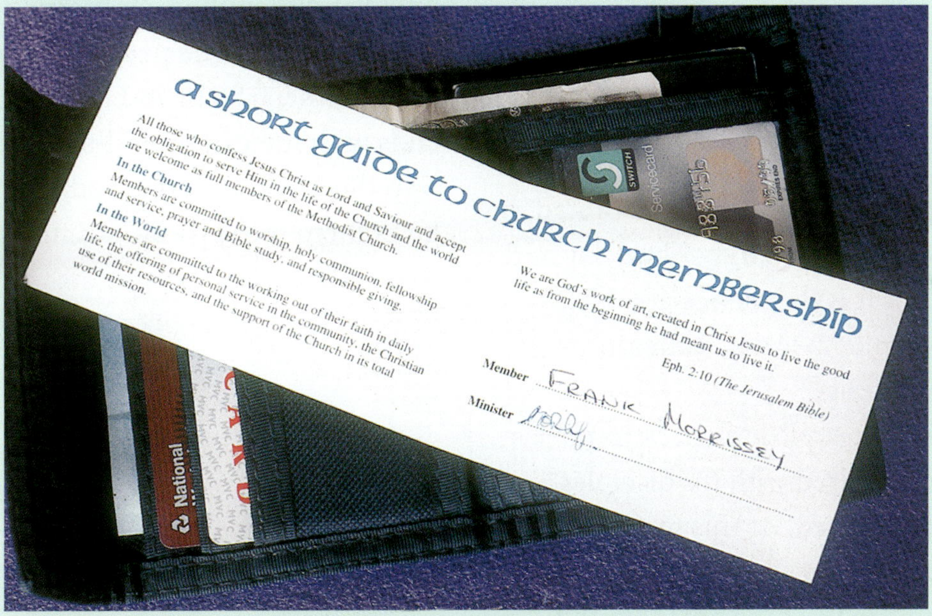

C *Why do you think that members of the Methodist Church sign this declaration at the start of every year?*

2 People who are confirmed are asked exactly the same questions that their parents and god-parents were asked when they were baptised. Can you think why?

Do you know?

- which Church baptises and confirms babies in the same service?
- who carries out confirmation services in Anglican and Roman Catholic services?
- what the laying-on-of-hands in the confirmation service means?

IN THE GLOSSARY

Anglican Church; Bishop; Confirmation; Holy Spirit; Infant Baptism; New Testament; Orthodox Church; Roman Catholic Church.

11 The Eucharist

In almost all churches Christians meet regularly for a special service. This service is called by many different names. To Roman Catholics it is the Mass whilst in the Orthodox Church it is called the Holy Liturgy. Nonconformist Churches, such as Baptists and Methodists, prefer to call it the Breaking of Bread or The Lord's Supper.

The Eucharist

The word 'Eucharist' means 'thanksgiving'. It is the most important service in Anglican churches. It is held every Sunday and at least once during the week. It is also celebrated on festival days, such as Maundy Thursday and Ascension Day. It is the service at which worshippers remember the death and resurrection of Jesus.

At this service people look back to the last meal that Jesus shared with his disciples before he was arrested. At this meal, often called the Last Supper, Jesus spoke about his coming death. He used the bread on the table to explain that his body would be 'broken' on the cross. The wine in the cup was used to show that his blood would be 'spilled'. Christians now remember that death by eating bread and drinking wine together.

The service

The Eucharist is a family meal in which all who have been baptised and then confirmed can share. Just before the bread and wine are blessed, people say to each other *'The Peace of the Lord be with you.'* This is called the Peace and people may shake hands or kiss each other. The people then come forward and kneel in front of the altar. They take the bread and then the wine from the priest or another server. The people reply each time, saying Amen (So be it, Lord). The service ends with the priest sending the people out into the world to serve God. The Eucharist gives them the spiritual strength to do this.

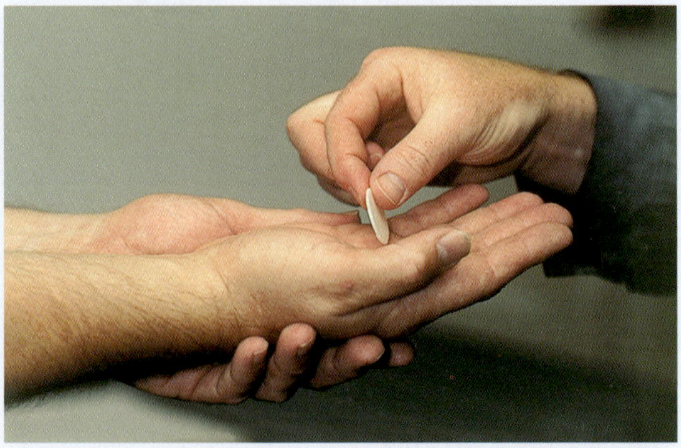

A *What does the piece of bread symbolise?*

B *What does this cup of wine symbolise?*

i INFORMATION BOX

'While they were eating, Jesus took bread, and gave thanks, and broke it, and gave it to his disciples saying,"Take and eat; this is my body." Then he took the cup, gave thanks and offered it to them, saying, "Drink from it all of you. This is my blood...which is poured out for many for the forgiveness of sins."' (Matthew 26.26–28)

- What did Jesus say was symbolised by the bread and wine?

? *Do you know?*

- the different names given to the most important Christian service?
- what the 'Peace' is?
- what Christians remember and celebrate at the Eucharist?

T THINGS TO DO

1 Think of the special things you might do to say thank you. Write a letter? Send flowers? Why is it important to say thank you? How do you feel if a friend forgets to say thank you?

2 a Why do you think that Anglicans call this service the 'Eucharist'?

b Why do you think this service is often called 'Holy Communion'?

3 Read the account of the Last Supper from Matthew 26.26–30, a part of which is in the Information Box. Re-tell this story in your own words.

IN THE GLOSSARY

Altar; Anglican Church; Ascension Day; Baptist Church; Breaking Bread; Disciple; Eucharist; Holy Liturgy; Last Supper; Lord's Supper; Mass; Maundy Thursday; Methodist Church; Nonconformist Churches; Orthodox Church; Peace; Priest; Roman Catholic Church; Sunday.

12 The Mass

In the Roman Catholic Church the service of Holy Communion is called the Mass. For this service the priest wears special clothes as you can see from photo A. This shows that the service is very important. The Mass always follows the same pattern. Worshippers follow it in their Missal, the Roman Catholic prayer book.

The Mass

The priest welcomes everyone to church with the familiar words:

'The grace of our Lord Jesus Christ, the love of God and the fellowship of the Holy Spirit be with you all.'

A *The bread used in the Mass is called the 'host'. Can you discover why?*

You have probably heard these words before. Everyone in church asks God's forgiveness for the sinful (wrong) things they have done. The priest sprinkles them with holy water to show that they have been forgiven. Three readings from the Bible follow and the last of these, from one of the Gospels, is always given by the priest from the middle of the church. The sermon (often called the homily) follows.

The people say the Nicene Creed. This expresses what the Church believes about God the Father, God the Son and God the Holy Spirit. After some prayers the money collection (called the offertory) is brought forward with the bread and wine for the Mass. The priest consecrates (makes holy) the bread and wine before giving them to the worshippers.

Finally, everyone in church is told to love one another and to go out into the world to serve God – and their neighbour. Sharing in the Mass must lead to the worshipper going out to help others. These two things are very closely linked.

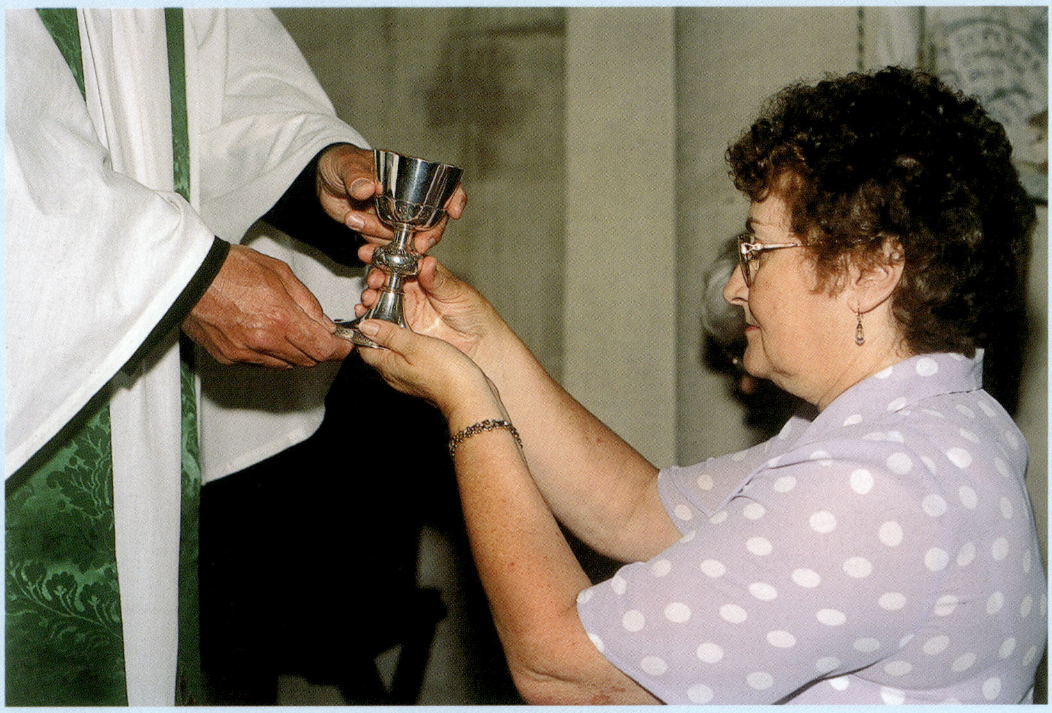

B *What are Roman Catholics reminded of when they drink the wine in the Mass?*

T THINGS TO DO

1 Write two sentences in your folder about the Mass.

2 During the Mass an offertory is brought forward. This includes money as well as the bread and wine for the Mass. The bread and wine are often carried in the service by children. Why do you think that children are chosen to do this?

3 Roman Catholics believe that Jesus is present in the Mass in a special way. Invite a Roman Catholic priest in to your class to explain to you just what Roman Catholics believe about the Mass. Have some questions ready to ask him about the service.

They have said:

John, 24: *'I have always tried to get to Mass as often as I can. The reason is simple. The service of Mass makes me feel comfortable. I can have my sins forgiven and share in the body and blood of Jesus.'*

- What is it about the Mass that makes John feel comfortable?

? *Do you know?*

- what the Mass is?
- where the service of the Mass is found?
- why priests wear special clothes for this service?

IN THE GLOSSARY

Bible; Gospel; Holy Communion; Holy Spirit; Homily; Mass; Missal; Nicene Creed; Offertory; Priest; Roman Catholic Church; Sermon.

13 The Holy Liturgy

In the Orthodox Church, Holy Communion is called the Holy Liturgy. The word 'liturgy' means an order of service. Over the centuries the order of service followed in the Holy Liturgy has become fixed. The service followed today was first used back in the fourth century.

A *Why do you think that the preparation of the bread and wine for the Holy Liturgy is done largely out of sight of the people?*

The Holy Liturgy

The bread and wine for the Holy Liturgy are prepared by the priest behind the iconostasis. The Royal Doors, in the centre of the iconostasis, are then opened and a procession moves around the church. The Gospels are carried high above the heads of the people as they sing three times: *'Holy God, holy and mighty, holy and immortal, have mercy on us.'*

The priests carry the bread and wine in the procession. They return through the Royal Doors and lay the bread and the wine on the altar. The people greet each other with the kiss of peace before saying the Nicene Creed. Everyone joins in the Lord's Prayer. The priest then lifts the bread high and breaks it.

IN THE GLOSSARY
Altar; Gospels; Holy Communion; Holy Liturgy; Iconostasis; Lord's Prayer; Nicene Creed; Orthodox Church; Priest; Royal Doors

The priest comes back through the Royal Doors and those receiving Holy Communion come forward and stand. The bread, dipped in wine, is put on a spoon and placed at the back of the mouth. Through this simple act each Christian is linked to everyone else who has shared in the liturgy – whether dead or alive. They have taken part in a service which gives them a picture of the worship being offered to God in heaven. The liturgy has given them a glimpse of God the Father, God the Son and God the Holy Spirit.

B *Orthodox Christians call this service the Holy Liturgy. What does the word 'liturgy' mean?*

They have said:

Alexis, Orthodox priest: *'The people who are going to take Holy Communion in our church gather together in the centre. Their hands are folded on their shoulders. The people stand as the chalice is brought to them. They simply open their mouths and the bread, dipped in wine and placed on a spoon, is put at the back of their mouth. It is important that no one touches the bread and wine. We believe that they are the actual body and blood of Jesus.'*

- How is the holiness of the bread and wine underlined – and why?

Do you know?

- what Holy Communion is called in the Orthodox Church?
- where the bread and wine are prepared for the Holy Liturgy?
- why the Holy Liturgy is important for Orthodox Christians?

THINGS TO DO

Here are six words used in this unit. The letters, though, are all scrambled up. Unscramble them and explain, in your own words, what each of the words mean.

1 GLYITRU

2 SCITNOSOSAI

3 TALRA

4 VEHNEA

5 YLAOR ORDOS

6 ENICNE RDECE

14 Breaking Bread

Churches like the Baptists and Methodists have their own way of celebrating Holy Communion. Some of them call it the Breaking of Bread. This title was used by the early Christians:
'On the Saturday night, when we gathered for the breaking of bread...' (Acts 20.7).

The Breaking of Bread

The communion table is placed at the front of the church – often in front of the pulpit. The minister sits behind the table with the deacons (leaders) of the church. On the table in front of them are trays with small pieces of bread and tiny glasses of wine. In the Breaking of Bread the bread is taken first. Each person takes a small piece and eats it immediately. This shows that everyone must respond to God for themselves.

The wine glasses are taken round but no one drinks until everyone has been served. This shows that everyone belongs to the one Church. A final prayer and thanksgiving end the short service.

In the Breaking of Bread service the bread and wine are just symbols. They prompt people to think about and remember the death of Jesus. As they eat the bread and drink the wine, the minds of everyone go back to the death of Jesus on the cross. The minister tells them to eat the bread and drink the wine, '*whilst feeding on him (Jesus) in your hearts by faith.*' That is exactly what they do as they break bread together.

A *In which church might you see a scene like this?*

T THINGS TO DO

1 Why do you think that Jesus left 'real' things, like bread and wine, for his followers to remember him by?

2 Look at the Information Box. The answer to questions a to e can all be found there. Questions f and g are a little more difficult.

- **a** What did God tell Paul – and what did Paul do with the information?
- **b** When did Jesus share his last meal with his disciples?
- **c** What did Jesus do after he had broken the bread in front of his disciples?
- **d** Why did Jesus tell his disciples that they should 'break bread' with each other?
- **e** Why should the disciples drink wine together?
- **f** Can you find out what the word 'covenant' means and then try to explain why it is used here.
- **g** How do Baptists and Methodists try to stick as closely as possible to the words of Paul?

3 The deacons take the bread and wine to the people. This teaches everyone an important lesson. What do you think this lesson is?

? *Do you know?*

- who helps the minister in the Breaking of Bread service?
- why the people eat the bread as soon as they receive it?
- why people wait until everyone has been given the wine and then drink it together?
- Why did Paul tell the Christians to eat bread and drink wine?

B *What is this person remembering as they take the glass of wine?*

i INFORMATION BOX

St Paul said that he had some special information from God:
'I received from the Lord what I also passed on to you. The Lord Jesus, on the night he was betrayed, took bread, and when he had given thanks, he broke it and said, "This is my body, which is for you; do this in remembrance of me". In the same way, after supper, he took the cup, saying, "This cup is the new covenant in my blood; do this, whenever you drink it, in remembrance of me."' [1.Corinthians 11.23–25].

IN THE GLOSSARY

Baptist Church; Breaking of Bread; Holy Communion; Methodist Church; Minister; Pulpit.

15 The Iconostasis

Almost every part of an Orthodox church means something important. Most churches are square with a dome over the centre. The square shape means that everyone is equal in God's sight. The four corners of the square represent the four Gospels whilst the dome is the heavens. The floor of the church stands for the earth beneath the heavens. In large Orthodox churches there is a painting across the ceiling showing Christ, the ruler of heaven and earth.

The iconostasis

Across the front of the church is a beautiful screen made of wood or stone. The screen comes between the altar and the people, between the nave and the sanctuary. The screen, the iconostasis, is covered with icons (sacred paintings) of Jesus, Mary (the mother of Jesus), the apostles and the saints. The word iconostasis itself means 'place of the icons', and these pictures help people to understand what God is like.

There are doors in the middle of the iconostasis (the Royal Doors). These are closed for most of the Holy Liturgy. The doors are opened when the priest leads the procession out with the bread and wine. There are special icons on either side of the Royal Doors. The one on the left shows the birth of Jesus, with the Virgin Mary seen holding the baby. The one on the right shows the return of Jesus in the future to the Earth.

The iconostasis is a very important part of every Orthodox church. The Holy Table (the altar) is the place where God is found. Only the priest, dedicated to God, is able to enter his presence at the altar. The priest brings that presence to the people when the Royal Doors are opened and he feeds them with the bread and the wine in the Holy Liturgy.

A *How would you describe this iconostasis to someone who had not seen it?*

B Why do you think there are icons on either side of the Royal Doors?

They have said:

John, 22: *'I have worshipped in a Russian Orthodox church for three years. When I first entered the church I was struck by its beauty. I was also struck by a sense of God's presence. The iconostasis is just part of that. It seems right to separate the Holy Table from the people. I know what I am like and I am beginning to understand what God is like.'*

- What do you think John means in his last sentence?

Do you know?

- what the iconostasis is?
- what the Royal Doors are?
- what covers the iconostasis?

THINGS TO DO

1 There are some blanks in this paragraph. Copy it into your book and fill in the missing words.

Most ______ churches are square in shape. This reminds worshippers that everyone is ______ in the sight of God. On the ceiling there is often a painting of ______. The ______ is an important part of an Orthodox church and is covered with ______. These are special paintings of ______, ______ , ______ and ______ .

2 The Royal Doors are in the middle of the iconostasis. Why do you think they have this name?

IN THE GLOSSARY

Altar; Apostle; Gospels; Holy Liturgy; Holy Table; Icon; Iconostasis; Nave; Orthodox Church; Priest; Royal Doors; Saint; Sanctuary; Virgin Mary.

16 Icons

Orthodox Christians believe that God is all-powerful. No matter how hard they try, human beings cannot worship him unless they are given some help. One of the most important ways of giving this help is through icons.

Icons

An icon is a special religious painting. You can see two of them in photos A and B. The painting may be of the Holy Family (Joseph, Mary and Jesus); the Virgin Mary with Jesus; Jesus as an adult; one of the apostles or a saint. Icons are not portraits. They try to bring God within reach of each worshipper. They are unique in the help they are able to give. Other paintings, however beautiful, cannot do this.

A *How would you describe this icon?*

B *How would you describe this icon?*

Each icon is a copy of a perfect image in heaven. To produce an icon is a very skilled task requiring many years of training. The painter of an icon prepares himself by prayer and fasting (going without food). The work itself is an act of worship. Bright colours are usually painted on wood although, sometimes, other materials are used. Icons are often decorated with jewels.

Using icons

Icons are most frequently found in Orthodox churches and homes. Worshippers usually light a candle in front of an icon and kiss the painting. In this way they are showing great respect for the holy paintings but they are not worshipping them. They are worshipping God the Father, Son and Holy Spirit (the Trinity) through the icons. Lighting a candle shows that the saints in heaven and on earth are one. Those on earth are looking to those in heaven for help and guidance.

They have said:

Dmitrou, 16: *'Painting an icon is a very special task. The artist uses special methods and colours. This makes the finished icon special. I have icons of two saints in my bedroom at home. I was given one of them when I was baptised as a baby. When I pray in front of an icon, at home or in church, I know that this person is listening to me in heaven.'*

- There are two important words in this description – icon and saint. Discuss these two words with the person sitting next to you. Write down everything they suggest to you.

Do you know?

- what an icon is?
- what figures are painted on the icons?
- how icons are used in worship?

THINGS TO DO

1 **a** What do you think a 'saint' is?

b Do you think there are saints alive today?

c Schools and colleges are often named after saints. What examples can you find in the area around you? Make a list and compare it with other people's in the class. Find out a little more about one of the saints on your list. Write a short description of the saint in your folder.

2 Have you ever met or heard of someone you would describe as a 'saint'? Write down your own description of them. Why do you think there are 'saintly'?

3 Imagine that you are the priest of an Orthodox Church. There has been a burglary in your church and thieves have escaped with two valuable icons. The police have asked you to supply them with drawings and descriptions of the icons taken. Draw two pictures and write two sentences about them in your folder.

4 When they go to an Orthodox church most people light a candle in front of an icon before they do anything else. Can you think of a reason for this?

IN THE GLOSSARY

Apostle; Icon; Joseph; Orthodox Church; Saint; Trinity; Virgin Mary.

17 The Rosary

Many Christians, mainly Roman Catholics, find it helpful to use a rosary ('rose-garden') in their prayers. Sometimes they use them in church but usually in their own private prayers at home.

The rosary

The rosary is a string of fifty beads (see photo A) made up of five groups of ten beads each. There is a single bead in between each group of beads. Attached to one of the single beads is a cluster of three beads, another single bead and a crucifix. A person can pass the beads through their fingers without needing to look at them.

A *Some Roman Catholics use a rosary regularly whilst others do not have one. Can you suggest one reason for this?*

In working their way through the rosary a person says three important prayers:

a **The Lord's Prayer.** Sometimes called the Pater Noster this prayer begins *'Our Father, who art in heaven…'*

b **The Hail Mary** (the Ave Maria). You can find this in the Information Box.

c **The Gloria Patri.** This short prayer begins 'Glory to the Father…'

The holy mysteries

As the person works their way through the rosary they are encouraged to think about different events in the life of Jesus. These start with 'five joyful mysteries' around the birth of Jesus before going on to 'five sorrowful mysteries' centred on the death of Jesus. Finally there are 'five glorious mysteries' including the resurrection of Jesus and the journey of Mary, his mother, into heaven at the end of her life. Each person will think (contemplate) about just one of these mysteries.

IN THE GLOSSARY

Ave Maria; Crucifix; Gloria Patri; Hail Mary; Lord's Prayer; Pater Noster; Roman Catholic Church; Rosary; Virgin Mary.

B *In this church a rosary has been wrapped around a cross. Can you suggest why?*

i INFORMATION BOX

This Roman Catholic prayer is called the Hail Mary:
'Hail Mary, full of grace,
The Lord is with you.
Blessed are you among women and blessed is the fruit of your womb, Jesus.
Holy Mary, Mother of God,
Pray for us sinners now
And at the hour of our death. Amen.'

- The Hail Mary says several things about Mary, the mother of God. What are they? You will find out more about the Virgin Mary in Chapter 23.

? *Do you know?*

- what a rosary is?
- which three prayers are said during the saying of the rosary?
- how many 'mysteries' are brought to mind during the saying of the rosary?

They have said:

Anna, 58: *'I have used the rosary since I was little. I don't have to think about the beads because I know my way around the rosary so well. I can concentrate my thoughts on God and the events in the life of Jesus.'*

- What events in Jesus' life does the rosary help Anna to think about?

T THINGS TO DO

1 You are a Roman Catholic. Your friend has no idea what a rosary is or what it is used for. What would you tell them?

2 a Read the Hail Mary. Now read Luke 1.26–38. Part of the prayer reminds us of the words spoken to Mary by the Angel Gabriel. Why did the two meet and what was Mary told?

b Why do you think that the Angel called Mary 'blessed' and what do you think he meant?

c Why do you think that Mary is addressed in this prayer as 'the mother of God'?

d How do you think that Roman Catholics might gain strength by praying to Mary?

18 A Place for the Bible

The Bible is the holy book for all Christians. It is divided into two parts – the Old Testament and the New Testament. The Old Testament is shared by both Christians and Jews. The New Testament is the part of the Bible which is most important to Christians.

Using the Bible

Most Christians read a part of the Bible every day. They set aside time for prayer and Bible-reading. They also listen to the Bible being read in every church service. You will find a Bible on the lectern (stand) at the front of most churches. The lectern often has the carving of an eagle on the front.

A *The eagle on the front of the lectern is often resting his claws on a ball. What do you think the ball might symbolise?*

During many church services there are three readings from the Bible. The first of these comes from the Old Testament. The second is taken from one of the letters, called Epistles, written by one of the early Christians in the New Testament. Although most of these were written by Paul, both Peter and John wrote more than one. The third reading, the most important, comes from one of the four Gospels in the Bible. These books describe the life, teaching and death of Jesus. There are two ways in which the importance of this reading is shown in many churches:

- **a** The Bible is carried in a procession to the centre of the church whilst the people stand. In the Orthodox Church it is carried above the heads of the people.
- **b** Whilst the other two readings can be taken by anyone, the Gospel reading is always given by a priest.

In Anglican and Roman Catholic churches parts of the Bible are also sung in many services. Two of the most well known parts of the story of the birth of Jesus are sung. Mary's song, the Magnificat, Simeon's song and the Nunc Dimittis, are an important part of worship. So, too, is the singing of Psalms from the Old Testament.

IN THE GLOSSARY

Anglican Church; Bible; Epistles; Gospels; John; Lectern; New Testament; Old Testament; Orthodox Church; Paul; Peter; Priest; Roman Catholic Church.

B *Why do you think that ordinary people are encouraged to take part in church services by reading from the Bible?*

They have said:

Andrew, 18: *'I have never found the Bible easy to read or understand. The Gospels are the most important to me. My life as a Christian begins and ends with Jesus. The letters of Paul, and others, are not easy. Everyone tells me, though, that they are important.'*

- Why do you think that Andrew, and other young Christians, find parts of the Bible difficult to understand?

Do you know?

- what the two parts that make up the Bible are called?
- where the three readings are taken from, that play an important part in many church services?
- how the importance of the reading from the Gospels is indicated in many services?

THINGS TO DO

1 Christians read the Bible because they find it helps them to live a Christian life.

- **a** Are there any books that you have found helpful to read? Explain why they helped you.
- **b** Why do you think that Christians turn to the Bible? What kind of help do you think they might find in it?
- **c** Read Luke 6.27–36. Put the verses into your own words. Can you think of two reasons why these verses might be very important to a Christian?

2 Look at photo A. It shows a lectern holding a Bible. Many lecterns have a carving of an eagle on them. Can you work out why this might be?

19 Preaching the Word

In many churches the most important part of a service is the preaching of 'God's Word', the Bible. This is true in all Baptist, Methodist and Salvation Army churches and citadels (see Chapter 35). The preaching, usually by the minister, takes place in the pulpit. Christians in these churches believe that God 'speaks' to them through the preaching of the Bible.

A *What is one reason why you will find a pulpit in all churches?*

The pulpit

The pulpit is a raised platform that stands at the front of the church (see photo A). Three or four steps lead up to it. The platform is enclosed and the minister standing in the pulpit can see out over the whole congregation. The outside of the pulpit is often beautifully carved with scenes from the Bible. The minister, who can be a man or a woman, stands in the pulpit to deliver the sermon.

Services in these churches are not taken out of a prayer book. The person leading the service decides the form it will take. Hymns (religious songs), prayers and readings from the Bible will certainly play a very important part. The sermon will be based on a passage from the Bible. The people will be told about the teaching of Jesus and what it means to be a Christian today. People sitting in the congregation may have their own Bible so that they can follow the sermon.

The sermon comes towards the end of the service. On Sunday mornings, when most of the people at the service are Christians, the sermon may last for half an hour or more. On Sunday evenings a special effort is often made to bring people who are not Christians to church. At these services the Gospel is explained and people are invited to become Christians. This service is called a Gospel service and is a special feature in many churches.

B *Some people think that a sermon is out-of-date. Why do you think they say this? Do you agree with them?*

They have said:

Anneka, 16: *'I go to a Pentecostal church. Our services are pretty lively, I can tell you. Everyone moves around to sing and dance in them. I enjoy all this. The part that I really like, though, is the sermon because this is a chance to be quiet and thoughtful. Our minister explains a part of the Bible in his sermon. In some of them he invites people to become Christians. I always pray that someone listening will accept Christ as their own Saviour. Often they do!'*

- Why does Anneka enjoy the sermon in her own church?

Do you know?

- what the most important part of a service is in many churches?
- what the pulpit is?
- what takes place in a pulpit?

THINGS TO DO

1 Your local Baptist or Methodist church has written to your school. They need a new pulpit and have asked your school to design it. Draw and design a new pulpit.

2 Answer each of these questions in your own words:

a What is the most important part of a Baptist or Methodist church?

b What is the sermon in a service likely to be about?

c Why do many people bring their Bibles to church with them?

IN THE GLOSSARY

Baptist Church; Bible; Citadel; Minister; Pulpit; Salvation Army; Sermon.

20 Seeking Forgiveness

Being sorry for doing wrong things (sins) is an important part of worship in every church. In some churches people confess their sins quietly as they pray to God. These prayers are known as 'prayers of confession'. In some churches people are given other opportunities to confess their sins.

A *What do you think a person might gain from confessing to a priest?*

Reconciliation

Orthodox believers, Roman Catholics and some Anglicans confess their sins privately to a priest. Roman Catholics go to 'confession' at special times of the year although they can also go at other times. They confess their sins in private to a priest. He is not allowed to pass that information on to anyone else.

There are confession boxes in some Catholic churches. A grille is placed down the middle to separate the priest and the person. The priest is not supposed to know who is the other side of the grille although he will, of course, often recognise their voice. In some churches though, the two people simply sit down and talk to each other.

The priest tells them that God will forgive their sins if the person is really sorry. He may suggest a penance (penalty), such as saying some prayers, to show God how really sorry they are. The priest places his hand on the person's head or shoulder and prays with them. This is called absolution.

The mercy-seat

Something similar takes place in a Salvation Army citadel. There is a place of forgiveness at the front called the mercy-seat. This is a platform at which all who seek God's forgiveness can kneel. Sometimes services end in a citadel with people being invited to come forward and do this. It is a symbol of God's kindness and forgiveness.

B *Why do you think that these people are seeking God's forgiveness in front of other people?*

They have said:

Alan, 15: *'I have been a Salvationist for as long as I can remember. The sight of people coming forward to the mercy-seat at the end of services is familiar to me. When I first did it, though, it churned me up a bit. I was not upset about anything I had done. I just wanted to commit my future life to God. It was a bit difficult in front of all those people but I am glad I did it. At least a lot of people in my citadel are now praying for me.'*

- What do you think coming forward to the mercy-seat meant to Alan?

Do you know?

- what 'confession' is?
- what 'absolution' is?
- what happens at the mercy-seat?

THINGS TO DO

1 a What makes you feel very unhappy – and sorry?

b Have you done something and then known straight away that it was wrong?

c When you have done something wrong does it help to talk it over with someone?

d Does it help if someone tells you that you have been forgiven for what you have done?

2 Christians believe that everyone makes mistakes as they travel through life.

a How do Roman Catholics say sorry to God for the wrong things they have done?

b How do members of the Salvation Army seek God's forgiveness for their sins?

IN THE GLOSSARY

Absolution; Anglican Church; Mercy-Seat; Orthodox Church; Penance; Priest; Roman Catholic Church; Salvation Army.

21 Reminders of a Death

For Christians the death of Jesus is the most important event in history. You will find reminders of that death in most churches. In Catholic churches, for example, there are 14 Stations of the Cross around the walls. These are sculptures or tapestries illustrating the places that Jesus stopped on his way to the cross. They play an important part in the worship of these churches on Good Friday. You can find out more about them and how they are used in Chapter 22.

A Here you can see a cross on a Communion table. Why is this an appropriate place to find a cross in a church?

The cross

There are crosses in most churches. The cross is the most important symbol of the Christian faith. In Baptist and Methodist churches it is likely to be a simple wooden cross placed on the Communion table at the front (see photo A). Christians often think about the death of Jesus. They believe that Jesus offered up his life to God so that people could have their sins forgiven. By dying, Jesus was paying for the sins of the whole world. This is almost impossible for people to understand. The many different symbols of the cross in church help them to see this more clearly.

The crucifix is a special kind of cross. Crucifixes are very common in Roman Catholic and Orthodox churches. A crucifix is a cross with the body of Jesus on it. Usually the figure on the cross is that of a dying man. Occasionally, however, you will find old crucifixes holding the figure of Christ, the king. This is to remind everyone that Jesus overcame death. After he rose from the dead he returned to his Father in heaven. This event is known by Christians as the 'ascension'. The death of Jesus is celebrated by Christians each year on Good Friday, and the ascension on Ascension Day.

B *What will you usually find on a crucifix and why is it there?*

? Do you know?

- some of the ways in which Christians remind themselves of the death of Jesus?
- what the Stations of the Cross are?
- what a crucifix is?

T THINGS TO DO

1 A crucifix reminds Christians of the death of Jesus. It also reminds them that there are many people who suffer in today's world.

a Design and draw your own crucifix in your folder.

b Draw or write things around the crucifix which 'wound' or 'hurt' you and other people.

2 It is surprisingly true that the early Christians, in the years following the death of Jesus, would not use the symbol of the cross in their worship in any way. Can you suggest two reasons why they might have been reluctant to do so?

IN THE GLOSSARY

Ascension; Baptist Church; Crucifix; Good Friday; Methodist Church; Orthodox Church; Roman Catholic Church; Stations of the Cross.

22 Stations of the Cross

Stations of the Cross are one of the most familiar, and important, parts of a Roman Catholic church. Quite soon after the death of Jesus, pilgrims from all over the world began to visit Palestine. This was the country where Jesus had lived and taught. The most important part of their pilgrimage was to visit Jerusalem, the city in which he died.

By the twelfth century, however, it was very dangerous to make this journey. The Crusades, in which Christian armies fought Muslims and Jews, prevented almost everyone from going. Instead, pictures were put up in church to remind people of the sufferings of Jesus. Soon almost every church had 14 of these pictures or sculptures.

A *What is happening in this Station of the Cross?*

Stations of the Cross

The 14 Stations of the Cross tell the story of the last few hours in the life of Jesus. They go from:

a the appearance of Jesus before Pontius Pilate, the Roman governor,
b through the three occasions when Jesus fell under the weight of the cross,
c to his death on the cross,
d to the placing of his body in the tomb.

Twelve of the Stations refer to incidents which are mentioned in the Gospels.

As you can see from photos A and B these Stations are often beautiful carvings, pictures or tapestries. Each Good Friday, the day on which Christians remember the death of Jesus, Roman Catholics walk around each of the Stations. They light a candle in front of each and say a thoughtful prayer before moving on to the next.

B *What is happening in this Station of the Cross?*

? Do you know?

- why Stations of the Cross were first put in churches?
- what story is told by the different Stations of the Cross?
- how Roman Catholics make use of the Stations of the Cross each Good Friday?

IN THE GLOSSARY

Good Friday; Gospels; Jerusalem; Pontius Pilate; Roman Catholic Church; Stations of the Cross.

T THINGS TO DO

1 There are words missing in each of these sentences. Copy the completed sentences in your folder:

a You will always find ______ of the ______ in every ______ ______ church.

b The Stations of the Cross show different places in the last few hours of the life of Jesus from ______ ______, the Roman governor, to the ______ in which his body was laid.

c Roman Catholics visit each of the Stations on ______ ______ and stop to ______ a ______ in front of each carving.

2 Four of the Stations of the Cross are mentioned in this chapter. Take just two of them. Design your own Stations of the Cross to illustrate them.

3 Between noon and three o'clock on Good Friday many Christians visit the Stations of the Cross in their church.

a What are the Stations of the Cross?

b In what churches would you find them?

c How many Stations of the Cross are there?

d List six events in the last few days of the life of Jesus which are shown in the different Stations of the Cross.

e What do people do when they stop in front of each of the stations?

23 The Virgin Mary

All Roman Catholic churches have a statue of Mary, the mother of Jesus (see photo A). Catholics call her 'Our Lady'. She is also given the title 'Mother of God' to show that she gave birth to Jesus, the Son of God.

A *This is a statue of the Virgin Mary. What do Roman Catholics and Orthodox Christians believe about her?*

Mary, the perfect example

When Mary was told by the angel Gabriel that she was to have a baby, she was young and unmarried. You can read about what happened next for yourself in Luke 1.26-38. As you can see Mary accepted the angel's word that she was to give birth to God's Son. She did this although she was not married. She accepted that the father of her baby would be the Holy Spirit. To Roman Catholics this makes Mary the perfect example for everyone to follow. She was humble and obedient to God. Every Christian should be like her.

Both the Roman Catholic and the Orthodox Churches share the same beliefs about Mary. Both believe that Mary:

- was born without any sin.
- was chosen by God to bear his Son, Jesus.
- gave birth to Jesus without any human father being involved.
- went straight to heaven without dying at the end of her life.

B *What do you think Roman Catholics mean when they call Mary 'Our Lady'.*

There are many icons in Orthodox churches which show Mary, usually with the baby Jesus. Roman Catholics, though, pray to Mary. They believe that she is in heaven at the moment praying to God for the souls of those who are still alive. Those on earth can pray to God through the Virgin Mary. She 'intercedes' (pleads with God) for them. The Church shows how grateful it is to her by dedicating more than one festival each year to her memory.

INFORMATION BOX

This is one prayer that Roman Catholics often use:
'Hail, holy Queen, Mother of Mercy! Hail, our life, our sweetness and our help. To Thee do we cry…to Thee do we send up our sighs, mourning and weeping in this vale of tears…show unto us the blessed fruit of thy womb, Jesus. O clement, O loving, O sweet Virgin Mary. Pray for us, O holy Mother of God, that we might be made worthy of the promises of Christ.'

- What do you think each of the titles for Mary in this prayer mean?

Do you know?

- who the Virgin Mary is?
- why the Virgin Mary is the perfect example for Christians to follow?
- how the Virgin Mary helps Roman Catholics today?

THINGS TO DO

1 a Look at photos A and B. Write a sentence describing what you can see.

b Why do you think that Roman Catholics find it helpful to pray in front of a statue of the Virgin Mary?

2 You have a friend who wonders why the Virgin Mary plays such an important part in Roman Catholic worship. Write a brief letter to him/her explaining what the importance of the Virgin Mary is to Roman Catholics.

IN THE GLOSSARY

Holy Spirit; Icon; Orthodox Church; Roman Catholic Church; Virgin Mary.

24 Holy Men and Women

Many Christians look at saints and see them as men and women who have lived very holy lives. Saints are those who have followed the example and teachings of Jesus in their lives. Usually, but not always, they have met a violent end. Their lives provide a clear example for others to follow.

In the Roman Catholic Church the memory of saints is particularly important. Roman Catholics offer prayers to the saints who have died. They believe that these people have influence with God in heaven and so can help people still living on earth. The most important of all the saints is the Virgin Mary as we saw in Chapter 23. Roman Catholics pray to her regularly.

A *This stained glass window shows a saint. Is there a church or school close to you which is dedicated to a saint? If so, try to find out five things about the saint.*

Saints

In the early days of the Church, Christians were often cruelly treated. Many Christians lost their lives. People who died in this way were very important in the memory of the Church. They were greatly loved and respected. Amongst the leading Christians put to death (martyred) were Peter and Paul. They were executed in Rome in 64 AD. Many churches are named after these two saints – as you can see in photo B.

Over the centuries many men and women have been thought to be particularly holy or brave. Whilst many of these saints are well-known others are known to just a few. The name of St Ia, for instance, is attached to some churches in Cornwall but to none elsewhere. This saint is believed to have sailed across the sea from Ireland on a leaf! It is very difficult to separate fact from fiction in the history of many saints. It is even doubtful whether some of them, such as St George, ever existed. People, though, have still found them inspiring. Every day in the Christian year is devoted to more than one saint. The holy people of the past still inspire Christians today.

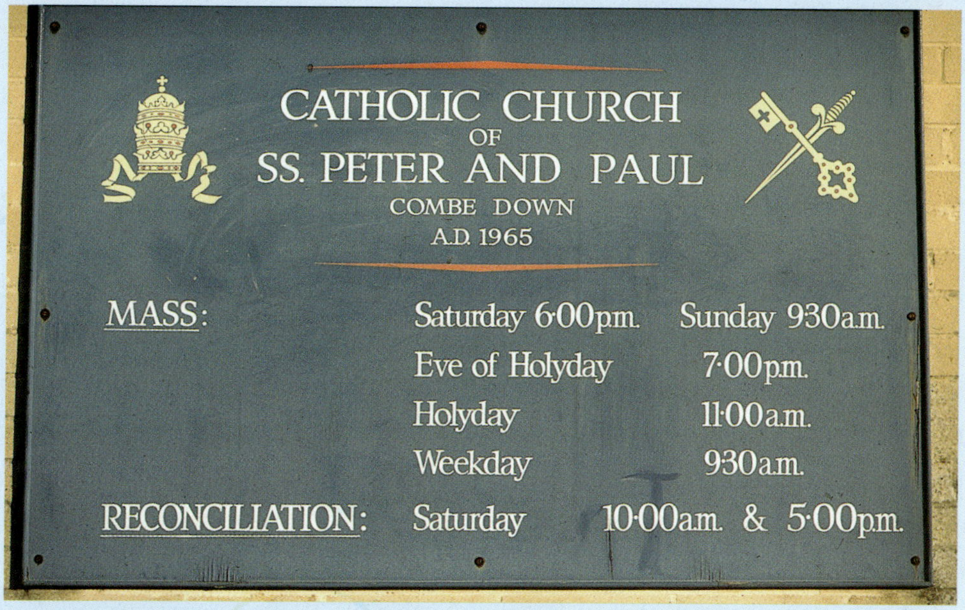

B *This church is dedicated to Peter and Paul. Most churches are dedicated to a saint or saints. Can you think of one reason why?*

? Do you know?

- what a saint is?
- which Church is particularly inspired by the saints of the past?
- why saints are still important to many Christians today?

T THINGS TO DO

1 The two parts of these sentences have been separated. Match them carefully and copy the completed sentences into your folders.

- **a** Saints are …
- **b** Saints have usually…
- **c** The Roman Catholic Church…
- **d** Roman Catholics believe that…
- **e** The most important saint to Roman Catholics…
- **f** Roman Catholics pray regularly…
- **g** Peter and Paul…
- **h** St Ia…

- **1** …values saints and their memory most highly.
- **2** …saints in heaven can pray for them.
- **3** …holy men and women.
- **4** …is the Virgin Mary.
- **5** …met a violent end.
- **6** …met their deaths in 64 AD.
- **7** …is believed to have sailed from Ireland to Cornwall on a leaf.
- **8** …to the Virgin Mary.

2 Select one of the saints mentioned in this chapter. Find out as many pieces of information about him/her as you can.

IN THE GLOSSARY
Paul; Peter; Roman Catholic Church; Saint; Virgin Mary.

25 Candles

One of the most important Christian symbols is that of light. This is why candles have always played an important part in Christian worship. In every Roman Catholic church you will find a stand of small candles (votive candles) for worshippers to light. The candles are placed in front of a statue of Christ, the Virgin Mary or one of the saints. The lighting of the candles, together with the prayers of the saint, are believed to make the person's prayer more effective.

Candles play a very important part in Roman Catholic and Orthodox worship. They:

- are lit on the altar at the start of a service to show that Christ is believed to be present in the bread and wine.
- are carried into church as part of the procession of priest and servers which opens a service.
- are carried in front of the Gospels, when they are taken to be read in the centre of the church, during a service.

A A votive candle is being lit. Can you find out what the word 'votive' means?

The Paschal candle

This is the most important candle. The Paschal candle is lit for the first time as Easter Saturday becomes Easter Sunday. In the weeks before this, worshippers have been thinking about the death of Jesus. They now look forward to celebrating his resurrection. As midnight approaches the church is totally dark. Then the Paschal candle is used to light the candles that everyone in church is holding. The church is soon filled with light. The message to everyone is that Christ is no longer dead, but alive!

The Paschal candle stands next to the font. It is lit for all services until Whitsun (Pentecost) and then whenever:

- a baby is baptised.
- a person is buried.

B *What do you think is the link between this banner and the use of candles in church?*

T THINGS TO DO

1 Liz goes to a baptism in her church. During the service a small candle is lit from the Paschal candle and handed to one of the parents. After the service Liz asks the priest why this happened. What do you think he might say to her?

2 There are several ways in which candles play an important part in Roman Catholic worship. Describe them.

3 a What are votive candles? Where would you find them?

b Look up the word 'votive' in a dictionary and write the meaning down in your book. Why do you think these candles are called 'votive candles'?

c Who lights a votive candle in a church and where are they placed when lit?

They have said:

Julie, 15: *'I like candles anyway. I always light one in my room when it gets dark. It makes the room seem so much more friendly. I find that in church as well. The candles tell me that God is not too far away and that Jesus is listening when I pray. I am also reminded that Jesus described himself as the Light of the world.'*

- What reasons does Julie give for finding candles in church helpful?

Do you know?

- what a votive candle is?
- why someone might light a votive candle in church?
- what the Paschal candle is?

IN THE GLOSSARY
Gospels; Orthodox Church;
Pentecost; Priest;
Roman Catholic Church; Saint;
Virgin Mary;
Votive candles; Whitsun.

26 A Wedding

Not all weddings are held in church. About a half of all the weddings in this country are conducted in a Registry Office. Each year though, about 200 000 couples do marry in a church. The wedding service is unlike any other church service. It is a legal ceremony as well as a religious service. The vicar or minister is also the registrar whose job is to make sure that the couple are legally married. At the end of a wedding service the couple, and two witnesses, sign the wedding register.

A *What do you think this couple will promise each other as they set off on their married life together?*

A church wedding

A church wedding takes place in the presence of God and in front of friends and relatives. The marriage is intended to last for ever. This is why the couple promise to love each other '*...until death us do part.*' Divorced people are only allowed to remarry in a few churches.

During the wedding service the bride and groom promise to love, honour, respect and care for each other. The couple promise to do this as they stand together at the front of the church. The Information Box tells you what vows (promises) are made. The groom places a ring on the finger of his bride although, in many weddings, the couple exchange rings. Every ring is a perfect, unending circle. A wedding ring is a symbol of a love which, it is hoped, will last for ever.

To Roman Catholics, and some Anglicans, marriage is a sacrament. It is, though, unlike the other six sacraments. In those the priest passes on God's blessing to the worshipper. In marriage, the man and the woman give each other God's blessing. That is why a Catholic wedding always ends with the couple sharing Mass together at the altar. No one else in the church takes the bread and wine.

INFORMATION BOX

During a wedding service the bride and the groom are both asked to make certain promises:
'N, will you take N to be your husband (wife)? Will you love him (her); comfort him (her); honour and protect him (her); and forsaking all others be faithful to him (her) as long as you both shall live?'

- Put these promises into your own words to show that you understand what they mean.

Do you know?

- why a wedding is different to other church services?
- which promises the groom and bride make to each other when they marry?
- who the most important witness at a church wedding is?

IN THE GLOSSARY
Altar; Anglican Church; Mass; Minister; Priest; Roman Catholic Church; Sacrament; Vicar.

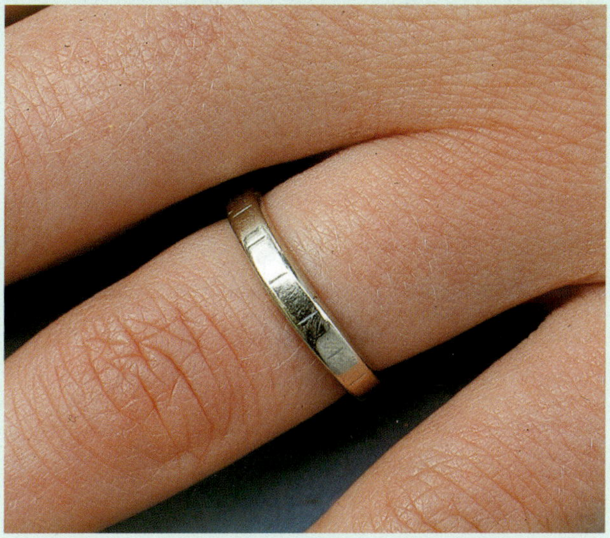

B *What does a wedding ring symbolise?*

THINGS TO DO

1 a Why do you think that almost all Christians want to marry in church?

b What do you think a Christian man and woman hope for each other as they stand together at the altar?

2 During a wedding service the bride and groom say these words as they place a ring on their partner's finger:

'I give you this ring as a sign of our marriage. With my body I honour you, all that I am I give to you, and all that I have I share with you, within the love of God the Father, Son and Holy Spirit.'

What do you think a person means when they say '*I give you this ring as a sign of our marriage*'?

27 Singing God's Praise

Most Christians enjoy singing. One of the first things you will notice in many churches is the organ. You can probably also see somewhere the pipes out of which the sound comes. St Paul told the early Christians to: '*...sing psalms, hymns and sacred songs; sing to God with thanksgiving in your hearts.*' (Colossians 3.16)

A *Why do you think that music has always played an important part in church worship?*

Hymns and sacred songs

Praising God has always been accompanied by music in church. In Old Testament times people sang and played instruments while they prayed. Many of these old songs are in the Bible. They are called psalms.

Psalms are sometimes chanted in church today. However, the singing of hymns is much more popular. More than one million hymns have been written in English alone. Some of them are very old. As most people in the past could not read or write, these hymns were learned off by heart.

Chants and modern songs

Many of the old chants, going back to the seventh and eighth centuries, are still popular. They are called Gregorian chants. Chants which come from a modern French community of monks, at Taize, are even more popular. Thousands of people, young and old, visit this community every year.

It was an old tradition that the singing in church was led by a choir. To begin with these choirs were all male. Gradually, though, women were allowed to become members. Today most choirs are found in large churches or cathedrals. Other churches may have a music group to lead their worship. Many modern hymns and songs have been written for groups like this to play. These new songs are particularly popular in Nonconformist and House Churches.

IN THE GLOSSARY

Cathedral; Old Testament.

B *Do you think that this is a good way to attract young people into church?*

They have said:

Peter, 13: *'I didn't use to like going to Mass but now I do. We have a music group which leads the worship and I get to play the drums with it. It means that I feel a part of the worship. I am making my own contribution. I also like the modern songs of worship more than the old hymns. They are more cheerful for a start.'*

- Why does Peter now enjoy going to church?

Do you know?

- which musical instrument is used in many churches to lead worship?
- the name given to the songs in the Old Testament?
- what a chant is?

THINGS TO DO

1 Most of us like to sing. We enjoy singing in a group.
  - **a** Describe three occasions on which people sing together.
  - **b** What kinds of things do they sing about?
  - **c** Why do you think people enjoy this?
  - **d** What are your favourite kinds of songs? Try to explain why.

2 Find as many different kinds of church music as you can on CD or tape. Your R.E. teacher or music teacher may be able to help you with this. Play the music in class and compare them. Which kind of music do you like most? Which kind do you like least? Explain why.

28 Windows and Banners

Stained glass windows in churches tell many different stories. They often show saints and martyrs from Christian history. Often the church itself is named after one of the saints shown in a stained glass window. Sometimes windows are a memorial to an important local person or to those who have died in battle.

A *Imagine that you have just seen this window for the first time. What impression do you think it might make on you?*

Usually, though, stained glass windows show scenes from the Old Testament or New Testament (see photo A). Popular stories, such as Adam and Eve or the Flood, feature in many of them. Prophets who looked forward to the coming of Jesus are shown preaching. Many stained glass windows show the infant Jesus with his mother, Mary. John the Baptist is often shown, especially in the churches named after him. The stories (parables) and miracles of Jesus are popular subjects too. Most popular of all, though, are the last few days in the life of Jesus, with his death on the cross and his resurrection from the dead.

Banners

Whilst modern stained glass windows are made for cathedrals and new churches, more and more churches are choosing banners to show events from the Bible. In many churches there is a banner-making group which make new banners for festivals and special occasions. The most popular festivals are Christmas, Easter and Pentecost.

You can see what a banner looks like in photo B. This one shows Jesus calling two of his disciples, Peter and Andrew, who were fishing at the time. The advantage of using banners like this is that they can be changed regularly. Their purpose is just the same as that of a stained glass window. It is to teach people about the Bible and the Christian faith.

B *Why do you think that many people, young and old, find banners an effective way of teaching about the Christian faith?*

They have said:

Alex, 14: *'In our church there is a stained glass window which has stunned me ever since I was a child. It shows God creating the world. The stunning part is that the sun often shines through the different fragments of glass as we are sitting there on a Sunday morning. Somehow the beautiful colours seem to fit perfectly with the beauty of creation.'*

- What do you think it is about stained glass windows, that make them one of the most beautiful parts of a church?

Do you know?

- what most stained glass windows show?
- what has replaced stained glass windows in many churches?
- which kind of events are often shown on modern banners?

THINGS TO DO

1 Look at photo A. It shows a stained glass window. Describe what you can see to someone who has not seen the window.

2 Look at photo B. It shows a banner illustrating Matthew 4.18–20.

   a It shows two people in the background. Who are they?

   b What are they doing?

   c What did Jesus say to them?

   d How did the words of Jesus change their lives?

IN THE GLOSSARY

Andrew; Bible; Cathedral; Christmas; Easter; John the Baptist; Martyr; New Testament; Old Testament; Parable; Pentecost; Peter; Prophet; Saint

29 Bishops and Priests

Roman Catholic, Anglican and Orthodox Churches have priests, although only the Anglican Church allows women to be priests. A person who is a priest, man or women, is said to be in Holy Orders. Each of these Churches also have senior priests called bishops.

Bishops

Bishops are priests who have responsibility for all the churches in an area, called a diocese. The cathedral is the most important church in the diocese and it is there that the Bishop's Seat is located. In the Roman Catholic Church, the Pope is the supreme leader of the Church although he is only a bishop, the Bishop of Rome. The Pope and the bishops of the Roman Catholic Church believe that they have taken over from the Apostles who were sent out by Jesus to continue his work. The leader of the Anglican Church is the Archbishop of Canterbury. There are many Orthodox Churches and each one of them is led by its own Patriarch.

A *This priest is wearing a dog-collar. Can you find out what this is – and why a priest wears one?*

Priests

A priest looks after one, or more, churches. At the beginning he, or she, is 'ordained' by a bishop. In a special service the bishop lays his hands on the priest's head and asks God's blessing for him or her. They are given authority to perform the sacraments. The area for which a priest is responsible is called a parish. In a large church the priest may be assisted by another priest who is called a curate.

A priest's spiritual authority varies from Church to Church. In the Roman Catholic and Orthodox Churches he is believed to represent the people to God and God to the people. In the Anglican Church he or she carries less authority. In all three Churches, however, only the priest can carry out the sacraments.

B *Many Roman Catholic priests are called 'father'. Can you find out why and why this reminds people of God?*

INFORMATION BOX

The Ordination Service in the Church of England describes a priest as:
'…called by God to work…as servant and shepherd among the people…to proclaim the word of the Lord…to declare the forgiveness of sins…to baptise….to preside at Holy Communion…to lead his people in prayer and worship…to minister to the sick, to prepare the dying for their death…'

- Describe, in two sentences, the work that a priest is called to do.

Do you know?

- what a bishop is?
- who the supreme head of the Roman Catholic Church is?
- what happens at ordination?

IN THE GLOSSARY

Anglican Church; Apostle; Archbishop of Canterbury; Bishop; Bishop of Rome; Cathedral; Curate; Diocese; Ordination; Orthodox Church; Parish; Patriarch; Pope; Priest; Roman Catholic Church; Sacrament.

THINGS TO DO

1 Some Churches do not have ministers or priests. Quaker services, for instance, are silent unless someone feels led by God's Spirit to speak. Can you think of one advantage and one disadvantage of this arrangement.

2 Look carefully at photos A and B. One shows an Anglican and the other a Roman Catholic priest.
   a What is distinctive about the clothes that the priests are wearing?
   b Why do you think priests wear instantly recognisable clothes?
   c Can you think of a situation in which you might want to talk to a priest? Why might you choose to speak to a priest rather than anyone else?

30 Ministers

One day Jesus began to wash the feet of his disciples. Peter protested that this was a job always done by the lowest servant in the household. Jesus told him:
You call me Master and Lord and so I am. If I, then, the Lord and Master, have washed your feet, you should wash each other's feet. I have given you an example so that you can copy what I have done for you. (John 13.14,15)

By doing this Jesus was setting an example to everyone who would be a leader in the church. He was reminding them that their main task is to serve other people, both inside and outside the church.

Pastors and ministers

Many churches recognise this when they call their leaders 'ministers'. Baptists have the same idea although they call their leaders 'pastors' – shepherds of the flock. These Churches do not have bishops. Instead they have Moderators or Superintendants who serve as church-leaders for a short period of time – often just a year.

Baptist churches elect members of the congregation to help the pastor of the church. These people are called deacons. One of the tasks of a deacon is to help the pastor conduct the Breaking of Bread service. They take the bread and wine to the people as they remain in their seats. Deacons, who can be men or women, also take services when the pastor is visiting another church.

Ⓐ *This Baptist minister is taking a church service. What are the main parts of his job?*

The Methodist Church often gives its ministers four or five churches to look after in his or her circuit. Ordinary church members are also trained to visit the different churches in the circuit to take services. These people are called lay-workers and they carry out many important tasks in all churches. You will find out more about lay-workers in Chapter 32.

B *Imagine that you are this minister. How would you try to serve the community in which you live – and your own church members?*

They have said:

Alex, 33: *'I have been a Baptist minister for five years. For two years before I went to college I was sure that God was 'calling' me to be a minister. I love the work that I am doing. I take two services every Sunday and sometimes speak at the Sunday School as well. During the week I spend time preparing my sermons. I also visit sick members of the church and pray with them. I take the weekly Bible-study and prayer-meeting. I sometimes take part in a programme on local radio. I live with my family in the manse, the Baptist equivalent to a vicarage.'*

- Do you think that the work of a minister and that of a priest are similar?

Do you know?

- why Jesus washed the feet of his disciples?
- why many church leaders are called 'ministers' or 'pastors'?
- what a lay-worker is?

THINGS TO DO

1 Why do you think the title 'minister' is particularly appropriate for someone who looks after a church?

2 Write one sentence to explain the meaning of:

a Minister.
b Pastor.
c Deacon.

IN THE GLOSSARY

Bishop; Breaking of Bread; Deacon; Disciple; Minister; Pastor; Peter.

31 Monks and Nuns

Almost from the beginning of Christianity there were men and women who dedicated themselves to God in special ways. Like Jesus before them, many took themselves off into the desert to follow a life of prayer. Before long, there were groups of monks living in monasteries and nuns in convents. Although their numbers have declined in recent years there are still thousands of monks and nuns – mainly in the Roman Catholic and Orthodox Churches.

Religious Orders

Monks and nuns live together in communities. They believe that they have a 'vocation' (calling) to this work. Each community belongs to a Religious Order. Everyone in the same Religious Order lives by the same rules. Three 'Rules' govern all religious communities:

a **The Rule of Poverty.** On joining a community a person hands over all their possessions. The community provides everything they need.

b **The Rule of Chastity.** Monks and nuns are not allowed to marry. They devote themselves to God and no one else.

c **The Rule of Obedience.** In a monastery the leader is the Abbot and in a convent the Mother Superior. Everyone obeys them.

A What do you think might have persuaded these monks to join a monastery in the first place?

B *Do you think that these nuns do an important job of work – for God and for others?*

These three Rules leave a monk or a nun free to serve God at all times. Their most important activity is prayer. They pray seven times a day starting in the early morning and finishing in the early evening.

Some religious communities are 'closed' having little contact with the outside world. Other communities are 'open' with monks and nuns working as teachers, nurses, social workers etc. Many communities are attached to Roman Catholic or Orthodox churches. They assist the priest in his many duties.

? Do you know?

- why some people choose to live as monks or nuns?
- what the most important work is for a monk or nun?
- what the difference is between open and closed communities?

T THINGS TO DO

1 Do you have a monastery or convent close to your school? If so, take the opportunity to invite a monk or a nun in to answer your questions. Work out what you are going to ask them in advance. Try to find out what life is like in a religious community.

2 a What are the three vows that monks and nuns take?

b Why do you think that these three vows were chosen?

c What problems to you think there might be in a community if the monks and nuns were not sworn to poverty, chastity and obedience?

IN THE GLOSSARY

Abbot; Convent; Monastery; Monk; Mother Superior; Nun; Orthodox Church; Roman Catholic Church.

32 Lay-workers

In every church much of the work is done by unpaid 'lay-workers'. These are men and women who carry out a wide variety of work ranging from cleaning the church to giving out the hymn books before a service. A church could not possibly survive without their help.

Lay-workers

There are some churches which do not have priests or ministers. The Quakers and the Plymouth Brethren are two such Churches. In these Churches the members share out all the responsibilities amongst themselves. They elect elders to look after the church and to recognise the 'gifts' which each member of the church has.

Lay-workers are essential in other Churches as well. In the Anglican and Roman Catholic Churches many people become Readers. This gives them the freedom to perform many of the tasks normally carried out by a priest, including taking services and giving sermons. Readers often take services in those churches which do not have a priest or are waiting for a new one to be appointed. Almost the only thing that a Reader cannot do is give Holy Communion. A priest alone can do this. Many churches without a vicar of their own use elderly, retired priests to conduct Holy Communion.

Behind the scenes much of the work in a church is carried out by lay-workers. Churches need to be cleaned and prepared each week for worship. Flowers and chairs must be arranged. Altars need to be laid with altar-cloths, crucifixes and candles. Candles need to be replaced and lit. Often members are needed to lead the worship by singing in a choir or music group. In the Church of England much of the leadership in each church is provided by the PCC (Parochial Church Council).

A and B (see page 67) Two jobs carried out by lay-workers in a church. Make a list of some of the other jobs that they do.

They have said:

Andrew, 29: *'I enjoy my involvement with my church very much. During the week I live a busy life but on Sunday I switch off and do anything at church I am asked to do. I have given out the hymn books, worked the P.A. system, made coffee and read the lesson. I honestly do not mind what I do. I just like to be involved – and serve God in my own way. I do not mind if people thank me or not. Mind you, its always nicer if they do!'*

- Why do you think that Andrew gains real pleasure from helping at church?

Do you know?

- what a lay-worker is?
- what a reader is?
- what kind of jobs a lay-worker might do in a church?

IN THE GLOSSARY

Altar; Anglican Church; Crucifix; Elder; Holy Communion; Lay-worker; Priest; Reader; Roman Catholic Church; Sermon.

THINGS TO DO

1 Here are five kinds of people you might find in any church. Can you think of any jobs in church that might be particularly suited to their skills?

a A school-teacher.
b A nurse.
c A politician.
d An electronics engineer.
e A singer.

2 Invite a local vicar or minister into school to discuss with you the part that lay-workers play in his or her church. Here are some questions that you might like to ask them:

a How important are lay-workers in your church?
b What are the most important jobs that they do?
c Is it difficult to get members of the congregation involved?
d Could the church function without their help and support?

33 Funerals

Christians believe that death is the gateway to a better life – a life that is everlasting. The body may decay and return to dust but the spirit, the most important part, lives on for ever.

Preparing for death

In some churches a person approaching death is prepared for it. The priest visits them in their home or hospital and anoints them with oil. He makes the sign of the cross with oil on their forehead. This is to comfort them. It assures them that God has forgiven their sins. They can now look forward to heaven. They also take Holy Communion for the last time.

The funeral service

In Roman Catholic families the coffin is taken to church and left there overnight. This allows people to pay their 'last respects'. Prayers are offered for the soul of the dead person. Catholics believe that dead souls spend time in purgatory being prepared for heaven, and that their prayers can affect the length of time they spend there.

The priest often wears white clothes for the funeral service. As he enters the church ahead of the coffin he says some words from the Gospels:
'I am the resurrection and the life; he who believes in me, though he die, yet shall he live, and whoever lives and believes in me shall never die.'

A *What do you believe about death – and life after death?*

In other churches it is believed that the soul of a dead person is committed to God's safe care. Passages are read from the Bible and prayers said. These encourage people to look forward to the end of time when they will all be reunited. Orthodox Christians believe that everyone, alive and dead, are part of the one Church. The coffin is left open during the service so that final goodbyes can be said. Pictures on white strips of John the Baptist, Mary and Jesus are laid across the dead person's forehead. An icon is placed in their hand. The body is covered with a cloth to show that it is under the protection of Jesus.

INFORMATION BOX

In many churches this prayer is said as the coffin is lowered into the ground:
'We entrust our brother/sister to God's merciful keeping and we now commit his/her body to the ground. Earth to earth, ashes to ashes, dust to dust; in sure and certain hope of the resurrection to eternal life through our Lord Jesus Christ, who died, was buried and rose again for us.'

- How can a Christian be sure that he or she will have eternal life?

IN THE GLOSSARY
Gospels; Holy Communion; Icon; John the Baptist; Priest; Purgatory.

B *Why are flowers on a grave a suitable symbol of life and death?*

Do you know?

- what Christians believe lives on after death?
- why a coffin is sometimes taken to church the day before a funeral?
- what is distinctive about a funeral in an Orthodox church?

THINGS TO DO

1 In the Roman Catholic Church the priest gives communion to people approaching death. He tells them that this is spiritual food for the journey ahead. What do you think the 'journey' is?

2 During the funeral service the priest likens a person's life to a flower that blossoms and dies, to a shadow that soon passes.

a Talk about these two 'pictures'. Do you think that they help people to understand life – and death?

b Can you think of another picture taken from everyday experience which might help explain life and death?

34 Reminders of the Afterlife

There are many reminders of a strong belief in life after death both inside and outside churches. In old buildings, especially cathedrals, there are often memorials on the floor or walls to people who have died. There may be elaborate tombs in which individuals, or whole families, were buried centuries ago.

Outside the church

A *A lych-gate at a church entrance. Why is it here?*

For a long time people were buried in church graveyards. Some still are but a lot of these graveyards are now quite full. They contain three reminders of the Christian belief that death is not the end:

a **Gravestones.** Until recently it was the custom to place a gravestone on every grave. Relatives waited about a year for the earth to settle and then included details about the person's life on a stone. In many crematoria there are walls with plaques in memory of those who have been cremated there.

b **Yew trees.** Yew is an evergreen tree which often lives to a great age. It has become an important symbol of everlasting life for this reason. It is frequently found growing in church graveyards. In the Middle Ages it was believed that the tree gave protection from evil forces. It was also thought to be unlucky to cut the tree down which is why so many are still standing.

c **Lych-gate.** In the past the coffin often had to be carried many miles to a church for burial. Lych-gates were built at the entrance to churchyards with seats or ledges on either side. The people carrying the coffin could then place it on one of the ledges to rest, before taking it on its final journey. The priest waited for the coffin here before beginning the prayers.

B *This gravestone shows a strong belief in life after death. Write down, in your own words, what it has to say.*

They have said:

Gill, 18: *'I have no real idea what heaven is like. Obviously the language in the Bible is a picturesque way of describing something that is beyond human language. All I know is that heaven is where God is – I am not too concerned about the details.'*

- Draw a picture or write a poem to express what you think about life after death.

INFORMATION BOX

The priest often reads these words from Psalm 103 at a funeral or cremation: 'The days of man are but as grass: he flourishes like a flower of the field; when the wind goes over it, it is gone: and its place will know it no more.'

- Put into your own words what this says about death.

Do you know?

- what reminders of a belief in life after death are found in many churches?
- why yew-trees are often found in churchyards?
- what lych-gates are and why they were built?

THINGS TO DO

1 In the story of the creation of the first man and woman in Genesis, God tells Adam: *'By the sweat of your brow you will eat food until you return to the ground, since from it you were taken; for dust you are and to dust you will return.'* (Genesis 3.19)

These words say something important about the Christian belief in life after death. What is it?

IN THE GLOSSARY
Cathedral; Priest.

35 Citadels

The Salvation Army is a Protestant Church which was formed in the middle of the nineteenth century. Its founder, Willam Booth, wanted to help the poor people in the new towns. He wanted to provide a place of safety for people from such evils as alcoholism and poverty. This is why he called his churches citadels.

He set up a religious organisation which he ran rather like an army. He called himself 'general' and there were also 'majors' and 'colonels'. Members wore uniforms that everyone began to recognise. Brass bands were formed to lead open-air services. Women members, wearing traditional bonnets, sold the Salvation Army newspaper, the *War Cry*, in pubs.

The Citadel

The Salvation Army does not hold Holy Communion or baptise babies. This is why you will not find an altar, communion table or font in a citadel. As you can see from photo A there is a place at the front of the citadel for the band and singers to stand. Music plays a very important part in the worship. The service is helped along by female singers, called songsters, who accompany the hymns by shaking their tambourines.

A *Do you notice any differences between this citadel and an ordinary church?*

There is a bench across the front of the citadel called the mercy-seat as we saw in Chapter 20. People kneel there to find God's forgiveness. The Salvation Army is the only Church to have its own flag. It carries the motto *Blood and Fire* and stands in the corners of the citadel. The Salvation Army crest is also to be seen in the citadel. Amongst the other symbols on the crest are a crown, the reward promised by God to those who are faithful, and a cross. Crossed swords lie across the cross to remind everyone that they are in a continual fight against evil.

They have said:

Annie, 18: *'I look upon the Salvation Army as my spiritual home. My parents are Salvationists and I have gone to the local citadel for as long as I can remember. I have always enjoyed the music and now I sing in a group. We take part in most services. It is my way of serving God. It gives a lot of pleasure to the people who come along to the citadel each Sunday.'*

- What do you think Annie means when she speaks of the citadel as her spiritual home?

Do you know?

- which kind of people the Salvation Army was set up to help?
- why Salvation Army places of worship are called citadels?
- what the mercy-seat is for in a citadel?

IN THE GLOSSARY

Altar; Citadel; Font; Holy Communion; Hymn; Protestant; Salvation Army.

B *How important is music in the worship in this Salvation Army citadel?*

THINGS TO DO

1. Explain why there is no altar, communion table or font in a Salvation Army citadel.
2. a Why do you think that the Salvation Army, alone amongst all Churches, has a flag and a crest?
   b Why do you think that the Salvation Army band carries the flag at its head when it is marching?
   c Why do you think the flag stands in the citadel when a service is going on?
   d Explain the meaning of two of the symbols which are found on the Salvation Army crest.
3. List three ways in which the Salvation Army is organised and run like an army.

36 Meeting-houses

Quakers are Christians who belong to the Society of Friends. This religious group, which started in the seventeenth century, does not have priests or ministers. From the beginning, Quakers wanted to show that they were not like other Christians. They adopted a particular style of dress. The men wore broad-brimmed hats which they refused to doff to anyone. They strongly believed that everyone was equal in God's sight. This belief still lies at the heart of Quaker worship today.

A *Why do you think that Quakers call their places of worship 'meeting-houses' rather than 'churches'?*

Meeting-houses

The buildings in which Quakers worship are called meeting-houses. Quakers do not celebrate any of the sacraments, such as Holy Communion and baptism. Their meeting-houses do not have an altar, communion table or font. The people do not sit in pews as they do in most churches. There is no organ or piano in a meeting-house since music does not play any part in Quaker worship.

Worship is instead conducted in a bare room with a table in the centre. On this table there is little more than flowers and an open Bible. The chairs are arranged around the table in a square or semicircle. In the few minutes before the hour-long service starts the people come and sit in their seats quietly. Silence is the key to any service in a meeting-house. The silence is only broken if someone feels that God's Holy Spirit is speaking to them.

The Holy Spirit is called the Inner Voice. The Inner Voice is God in every person and can only be found through silent prayer. Quaker meetings are designed to help people find God for themselves. A clerk is appointed for the meeting and he or she records everything that is said and done.

T THINGS TO DO

1 Silence lies at the heart of Quaker worship.

a Do you have silent moments in your life?

b What do you do in those silent moments? Are they important?

c Do you think that these moments are the times when God is most likely to speak to you?

d If silence is so important why do you think most church services are filled with noise?

2 In this paragraph some words are missing. Copy the paragraph into your folder and fill in the missing words:

The ______ are also known as the ______ ______ ______. They hold their times of worship in ______ ______. They do not have any ______ or ______ to lead their worship. Instead the people wait until the ______ ______ speaks to them.

3 When George Fox started the Quakers, he did not want it to be like any other Christian group or church. That is why their places of worship are called 'Meeting Houses.' List five ways in which Quakers are different to other Christian Churches.

? *Do you know?*

- what lies at the heart of all Quaker worship?
- what the Inner Voice is and what part it plays in Quaker worship?
- how God is experienced in a Quaker meeting?

B *How do these people meeting for worship hope to hear the 'Inner Voice'?*

" They have said:

Ben, 32: *'I became a Quaker three years ago. I live a high-powered life as an advertising executive and I found myself stressed out at the end of each week. I needed a form of worship that would recharge my batteries. I did not need noise – I have plenty of that each day. I went with my friend to the local meeting-house. It was bliss to sit there quietly for an hour each Sunday. Gradually I began to hear God speaking to me.'*

- Do you think that everyone would benefit from a time of peace and quiet every week?

IN THE GLOSSARY

Baptism; Bible; Holy Communion; Holy Spirit; Inner Voice; Meeting-houses; Minister; Priest; Quakers; Sacrament; Society of Friends.

Glossary

Abbot: The monk who is the leader of a monastery.

Absolution: The forgiveness of sins.

Altar: The holy table in a church where the bread and wine for Holy Communion are blessed.

Andrew: One of the disciples of Jesus, the brother of Peter.

Anglican Church: Worldwide group of Churches based on the teachings of the Church of England.

Apostle: Name given to the disciples of Jesus after the death and resurrection of Jesus.

Archbishop of Canterbury: Leader of the Anglican Church.

Ascension Day: The day, 40 days after Easter, celebrating the journey of Jesus into heaven.

Ave Maria: Prayer addressed to the Virgin Mary, used by Roman Catholics.

Baptist Church: The Church which only baptises adults.

Baptistry: The place at the front of a Baptist church where adults are baptised.

Believer's Baptism: Baptist Church's practice of only baptising adults who believe in Jesus.

Bible: The holy book of the Christian Church.

Bishop: An important priest in the Anglican and Roman Catholic Churches.

Bishop of Rome: The official title of the Pope.

Blessed Sacrament: The bread and wine in the Roman Catholic Church which have been blessed by a priest.

Breaking of Bread: Term used in many Nonconformist Churches to describe Holy Communion.

Cathedral: The main church in a diocese.

Chapel: A small Nonconformist church or part of a large church.

Christmas: The festival at which Christians celebrate the birth of Jesus.

Church of England: The established (official) Church in England.

Citadel: The Salvation Army place of worship.

Confirmation: Ceremony which follows baptism in Anglican and Roman Catholic churches.

Convent: The place where nuns live.

Crucifix: Cross carrying the image of dying Jesus.

Curate: A priest who helps a more experienced priest in a church.

Deacon: Person elected to be part of a team running a Baptist church.

Diocese: The area for which a bishop is responsible.

Disciple: A follower of Jesus.

Easter: The festival at which Christians celebrate the death and resurrection of Jesus.

Elder: A leader in some Nonconformist churches.

Epistles: Letters written by followers of Jesus and included in the *New Testament.*

Eucharist: Word used for Holy Communion in Anglican Church.

Extreme Unction: The anointing with oil in Roman Catholic churches as a person approaches death.

Font: The stone basin used for holding water for Infant Baptism.

Gloria Patri: A Roman Catholic prayer.

Good Friday: The day on which Christians remember the death of Jesus.

Gospels: The books by Matthew, Mark, Luke and John which open the *New Testament.*

Hail Mary: Important Roman Catholic prayer addressed to the Virgin Mary.

Holy Communion: The service at which Christians remember the death of Jesus.

Holy Liturgy: The service of Holy Communion in the Orthodox Church.

Holy Spirit (Ghost): The third person in the Christian Trinity – God the Father, God the Son and God the Holy Spirit.

Holy Table: The altar from which the Holy Liturgy is conducted in an Orthodox church.

Homily: Sermon given during a service in a Roman Catholic church.

Hymn: A song sung by a congregation in church.

Icon: Holy paintings of Mary, Jesus or the saints used in Orthodox worship.

Iconostasis: The screen, covered with icons, at the front of an Orthodox church.

Infant Baptism: Practice in Anglican, Roman Catholic and Orthodox churches of baptising babies.

Inner Voice: The way in which Quakers believe that God speaks to a man or a woman.

Jerusalem: The city in which Jesus died.

John: The writer of one of the Gospels and one of the disciples of Jesus.

John the Baptist: The person who prepared people for the coming of Jesus.

Joseph: The human father of Jesus.

Last Supper: The last meal that Jesus ate with his disciples before he was arrested.

Lay-worker: Anyone who does unpaid work in a church.

Lectern: The ledge used to hold the Bible in a church.

Lord's Supper: Title used by some Nonconformist Churches for Holy Communion.

Martyr: Someone who dies for their religious faith.

Mass: The Roman Catholic service of Holy Communion.

Maundy Thursday: The day before Good Friday.

Meeting-houses: Quaker places of worship.

Mercy-seat: Place to kneel for those seeking God's forgiveness in a Salvation Army citadel.

Methodist Church: One of the largest Nonconformist Churches.

Minister: The leader of worship in a Nonconformist church.

Missal: The Roman Catholic Prayer Book.

Monastery: The place where monks live and worship.

Monk: A man who devotes his life to God, lives in a monastery.

Mother Superior: The nun who leads other nuns in a convent.

Nave: Passageway down the centre of a church, leading from font to sanctuary.

New Testament: Second part of the Bible, contains Gospels and Epistles.

Nicene Creed: A fourth century statement of belief.

Nonconformist Church: Churches such as Methodist and Baptist, which do not 'conform' to the teachings of the Church of England.

Nun: A woman who devotes herself to God, lives in a convent.

Offertory: Collection of money offered to God during service.

Old Testament: The Christian word for the books of the Jewish Scriptures, first part of Bible.

Ordination: The service at which people become priests and so are able to give the sacraments.

Orthodox Church: A family of different Churches, largely found in Eastern Europe, the Middle East and Greece.

Parable: Story told by Jesus to illustrate a spiritual truth.

Parish: Local areas which have their own (Anglican) church.

Pastor: Name often given to minister in a Baptist church.

Pater Noster: The first two words of the Latin version of the Lord's Prayer.

Patriarch: Senior priest in Orthodox Church.

Paul: Important leader in the early Christian Church, writer of many epistles in New Testament.

Peace: The part of an Anglican or Roman Catholic service in which people pass God's peace to each other.

Penance: Penalty imposed in Roman Catholic Church before a person's sins can be forgiven.

Pentecostal Church: A Nonconformist Church.

Peter: A leading disciple of Jesus.

Pontius Pilate: Roman governor who condemned Jesus to death.

Pope: The leader of the Roman Catholic Church.

Priest: Person who conducts worship in many churches.

Prophet: A person sent by God to deliver His message.

Protestant Churches: Churches which are not Roman Catholic or Orthodox.

Pulpit: Raised platform in church from which sermon is given.

Purgatory: Place which Roman Catholics believe is between heaven and hell.

Quakers: A Christian denomination started in the seventeenth century by George Fox.

Reader: Someone who can take services in an Anglican church.

Roman Catholic Church: The largest Christian Church, led by the Pope in Rome.

Rood Screen: Screen which used to be in most Anglican and Roman Catholic churches between the altar and the people.

Rosary: Beads on a string used by Roman Catholics to help them pray.

Royal Doors: The doors in the middle of the iconostasis in an Orthodox church.

Sacrament: Christian service believed to carry God's special blessing to a person.

Saint: A man or woman recognised by the Church for their holiness.

Salvation Army: Protestant organisation started by William Booth.

Sanctuary: The area around the altar in a church.

Sermon: The part of a service where the Bible is explained.

Society of Friends: Another name for the Quakers.

Stations of the Cross: Sculptures in a Roman Catholic church showing places linked with the death of Jesus.

Stoup: Container inside the door of a Roman Catholic church containing holy water.

Sunday: The holy day for Christians.

Tabernacle: Cupboard which holds the Blessed Sacrament in many churches.

Trinity: Christian belief in God the Father, God the Son and God the Holy Spirit.

United Reformed Church: A Nonconformist Church.

Vicar: A person, man or woman, who conducts services in an Anglican church.

Virgin Mary: The mother of Jesus.

Votive candles: Candles which are lit when a prayer is offered in a Roman Catholic church.

Whitsun: Christian festival to celebrate the giving of the Holy Spirit, also called Pentecost.

Index